T0372508

Parents at Work

'Mark Gatto's book is a tour de force in the use of dystopian-fiction-informed critical discourse analysis integrating fiction and ethnographic experiences of working parents in patriarchal organisations. It offers both insightful and gripping counternarratives and deserves to be read widely.'
—Mark N. K. Saunders, Professor of Business Research Methods, University of Birmingham Business School, UK

'Confronting the patriarchal character of organisations, Mark Gatto's book offers a productive new way of understanding and ultimately addressing the discrimination and inequities that arise from being a parent at work. This is the first book of fictocriticism written in the broad fields of management and organisation studies, and this creative methodology has produced a compelling as well as educative text that will serve as a model for others.'
—Carl Rhodes, Professor of Organization Studies and Dean, UTS Business School, University of Technology Sydney

Mark Gatto

Parents at Work

A Dystopian 'Fictocriticism' to Subvert
Patriarchal Organisations

Mark Gatto
Northumbria University
Newcastle upon Tyne, UK

ISBN 978-3-031-15481-2   ISBN 978-3-031-15482-9   (eBook)
https://doi.org/10.1007/978-3-031-15482-9

Cover pattern © Melisa Hasan

This Palgrave Macmillan imprint is published by the registered company Springer Nature Switzerland AG.
The registered company address is: Gewerbestrasse 11, 6330 Cham, Switzerland

Acknowledgements

My first thank-you is to my wife and best friend, Holly, for all her love, support and encouragement. Without her by my side, I know this would not have been possible. She has given me the confidence to achieve something I never thought I could do. More important, during this journey, we became parents and have experienced the reality of parenthood together.

My second thank-you is for my mentor and friend, Professor Jamie Callahan, who made this project possible. Throughout our working relationship, I have developed immeasurably as an academic. I look forward to working with Jamie in the years ahead. I also want to thank Dr Rosemary White for her invaluable contribution in guiding my integration of dystopian fiction and masculinities theory.

I am especially grateful to the research participants who joined me on this journey. It was an honour to learn about their expectations and experiences of parenthood and I am grateful for their honesty, candour and trust. I wish them all prosperity and happiness.

My final thanks are to my family, without whom I would not be the person I am today. Special thanks to my parents, Ian and Gill, who gave me the foundations of love, respect and care. My parents-in-law, John and Alison, have always encouraged me to talk about my research and explain my ideas. I also want to thank my brother for his role in opening my mind to the spectrum of masculinities from an early age. Finally, thanks to my cousin, Rachel Hunter, for creating two wonderful pieces of art (Images 3.1 and 3.2) for the dystopian fictocriticism.

CONTENTS

ABOUT THE AUTHOR

Mark Gatto is an Assistant Professor in Critical Organisation Studies at Northumbria University. His main research interest is the gender inequity exacerbated by parenthood in paid employment, and the influence of masculinities (hegemonic, hybrid and caring). He is passionate about social justice and contributes to equity, diversity and inclusion initiatives in his place of work. Mark uses fiction as a subversive means of writing differently such as his HRDI paper 'Parenthood Demands: Resisting a Dystopia in the Workplace'. He has discussed his work in webinars and events exploring gender and methods.

Mark established the Northumbria University Parents and Carers Network in 2020 and is currently co-investigating a BA Leverhulme-funded project to better understand how such networks operate differently across the UK university sector. Early findings are summarised in this blog article at https://wonkhe.com/blogs/can-parents-and-carers-networks-help-make-academia-more-humane/. He is the volunteer treasurer of the cooperative Childsplay Nursery Ltd. and learns daily about the importance of community in early years' education and childcare. Mark also works with the Fatherhood Institute to promote involved fatherhood, including through the podcast series *The Daddy Leave Diaries* (https://anchor.fm/daddyleave) which catalogues his experiences of shared parental leave in 2022. He additionally contributed to a discussion of flexible work on the BBC Woman's Hour.

Mark lives in the North East of England with his wife and two children and enjoys family time in the outdoors.

LIST OF IMAGES

Introduction: Being a Parent at Work—Inhabiting 'In-Between' the Past, Present and Future

There ought to exist for the human being, in so far as [they are] conscious of being, a certain mode of standing opposite [their] past and [their] future, as being both this past and this future and as not being them. (Sartre, 2003, p. 29)

Abstract This chapter introduces the embodied experience of being and becoming a 'parent at work', and explores the 'writing differently' agenda in critical management/organisation studies. Drawing on lived experience and allyship to form an ethics of care, the chapter progresses from the personal and temporal elements of parenthood to better understand how such experiences can be articulated in different forms. The purpose of this chapter is to introduce and explore writing differently and fictocriticism as an appropriate method of research for affective topics that demand reflexivity, relatedness, responsibility, resonance and resistance.

Keywords Parents • Work • Organisations • Writing differently • Fictocriticism

There were many ghost versions of this book, written by spectral waifs of my former, present and future being, all of which have withered, decayed, fizzled out or disappeared without a trace. Writing about being a parent at

work is an act of defiance against the expectation of a detached, dehumanised, disembodied and masculinised scientific academic discourse. There is
no distilled truth I can offer to answer the question of the patriarchal
organisation for parents at work, to attempt such a task would obfuscate
the uncomfortable complexity of parental lived experience (my own and
fellow parents'). 'Parents at work' is an intentionally ambiguous title that
draws on socialist feminist arguments for the recognition and revaluing of
unpaid labour (Federici, 2021). In this book, work is presented as bound-
aryless as the mode of paid work is often infused with the ghost of unpaid
emotional labour (Hochschild, 1979), while the unpaid care work of parenthood is often blighted by daemons from cognitive paid work. Amidst
this frayed existence, parents are often merely surviving and performing a
self that passes as the 'ideal worker' in both roles. In this book, I enter into
a reflexive dialogue with the past, present and future, traversing the seam
(De Cock & Land, 2006) of 'fiction' and the 'reality' of the 19 parents'
stories I have translated as part of this fictocriticism, and my own lived
experience. Before I enter into this dialogue, I must state my positionality
as it will, undoubtedly, colour any reading of this text:

I AM A PARENT AT WORK.

I AM A PRIVILEGED, STRAIGHT, ABLE-BODIED, WHITE, CIS-GENDER,
MAN.

I LIVE AND WORK IN A WEALTHY, WESTERNISED
COUNTRY.

I LIVE A COMFORTABLE LIFE.

BUT

I FEEL THE PAIN OF PARENTS AT WORK.

AND

I KNOW THAT MANY PARENTS ARE STRETCHED TO
BREAKING POINT.

**THEY EXIST AND WORK THROUGH A DAILY SELF-NIHILATION
OF THEIR**

**BEING TO SERVE THE VORACIOUS HUNGER OF
THE PATRIARCHAL ORGANISATION.**

**I WRITE THIS BOOK IN SOLIDARITY WITH PARENTS AT
WORK TO DISRUPT AND SUBVERT MASCULINISED WORK
AND ACADEMIA.**

BEING A PARENT AT WORK

As a parent at work, I am obliged to accept a diminished version of my 'ideal worker' (Connell, 2005) self. I am truncated and manage the perpetual nihilation of my being as a writer and parent. This is not constructive of a better, leaner, cleaner version; I am no more refined as a writer than I am a consistently nurturing, 'authoritative parent'. In reflecting upon my own experiences of being a parent, I found myself drawn to Sartre's (2003) theorisation of *Being and Nothingness* as an abstract and fragmented exploration of consciousness. The nothingness I generate through necessary prioritisation of my daily life, be this through unanticipated illnesses, competing deadlines, or emotional exhaustion, dissipate as ghost versions of my former self. However, I am constantly reminded of such nihilations through the physical manifestation of a daily crackling knot in my right shoulder muscle (a snapping noise I can hear now as I type), the scar from an avocado injury on my left hand (an injury incurred in the month preceding the birth of my daughter while rushing to prepare dinner), and the persistent ache in my lower left back (an occupational hazard of writing and lifting children). This book represents a version of my being that is **only** one version of the many possibilities I could have offered as a product of the mostly unpredictable, occasionally incandescent and frequently exhausting reality of life as a parent at work.

I wrote this book before, during and after the birth of my daughter, which made me a second time father. I have learned a huge amount about 'being' a parent at work in the last year and I expect my experiences will continue to be as challenging, exasperating and rewarding as they have been so far. Alongside my wife, Holly, I am a parent to a one-year-old girl and a four-year-old boy (as of February 2022). In the process of writing this book, I have taken two spells of parental leave (totalling six months), visited the hospital five times with illnesses and accidents affecting Holly, and our son. As I write at the start of 2023, my family has just emerged from a serious bout of scarlet fever, followed by gastroenteritis, and I anxiously await the next virus to come knocking on our door.

As a parent, I often fleetingly inhabit the present amidst the competing demands of family life, and a melee of reflections of my paid working day, alongside ideations of my future. Whether it is planning a lecture as I walk down the stairs holding a baby in one arm and a bundle of dirty laundry in the other. Or, while on parental leave, feeding my daughter while checking emails (unpaid) on my phone, and listening to an audiobook of

Q by Christine Dalcher. It is in these swirling discursive moments that the 'work' of parenthood is most immediate, yet least tangible.

Existing as a parent at work necessitates a tumultuous relationship with the passage of time, and this fascinates me. I have been obsessed with speculative futures for as long as I can remember, from *Star Trek* to *Interstellar* and a plethora of dystopian fictions. It is partly the science fiction aspects that excite me, but also the social experimentation and critical, creative reflection on our past and present that is uniquely special about this genre (Cavalcanti, 2003; Stock, 2016). Though set in the future, these fictions are emphatic studies of our existing societies (Atwood, 2017) and the many human experiences that pass down from parent to child. It is the many possible futures awaiting us that haunt me when interacting with everyday life. As a parent, these futures become ever more chilling when considering what lies beyond my lifespan and will await my children. Do we stumble towards a nightmarish dystopia of conflict and global catastrophe, an inclusive utopia where technology solves the problems of injustice, or are we destined to regenerate endless hybrid 'ustopias' (Atwood, 2011) that simultaneously thrill and oppress selective groups? This book will not answer these questions, but it will create a speculative future and invite you to reflect on your experiences of inhabiting the in-between temporality of the past, present, and future of parenthood at work. My hope, in writing this, is to resonate with an academic readership who also are, one day will be, or see themselves as allies to parents at work. Through resonance, my intention is to evoke discomfort, affective solidarity and action.

BEING A WRITER

I describe this book as a dystopian fictocriticism within the academic genre of 'writing differently' (Gilmore et al., 2019; Grey & Sinclair, 2006; Pullen et al., 2020), which I have grown to understand as a feminist, anti-elitist, unconventional, embodied, humane, caring, resonant, rigorous, genre-bending, gender non-conformist, non-linear vanguard of contemporary academic writers in the field of Critical Management / Organisation Studies (CMOS). I write to contribute to a growing 'genre' of academic writing that includes the poetic, polemic, post-structural, autoethnographic, radical and fictional. I enclose 'genre' in ironic quotations to illustrate the genrelessness of this genre. Such a confounding pseudo-definition is consistent with my interpretation of the mission of this 'mode' of academia, to subvert the foundations of the field of CMOS and claim a space for historically othered voices within academia. I confess that my version of writing differently represents sometimes discordant fragments of this writerly agenda as a product of the many versions of me that have ceased to exist along the way. As a consequence, I have integrated my embodied self in ways I never originally intended, delved cautiously into the genre of genre-bending, and forayed into existentialist thought and temporality. I have written myself into this text, while also respecting the integrity of the voices that I have endeavoured to amplify through my fictionalised 'dystopian fictocriticism' as an in-between genre of writing that melds academic theory, empirical research (qualitative interviews with 19 participant parents), critical discourse analysis (Gatto & Callahan, 2021) and fictionalisation.

The 'in-between' that I introduce here is my attempt to approximate Sartre's concept of 'nothingness' (Sartre, 2003), which I have been drawn to since embarking on research that uses dystopian fiction. My parental experience of 'nothingness' includes the intangible ideas that swim around my mind, amidst a swirling shoal of everyday tasks like loading the dishwasher, tidying up the kitchen, and driving to the nursery pickup. Sentences form in seemingly perfect precision before fizzling out as I flail around the vestiges of my consciousness. I can occasionally clutch at them, sometimes even indulge a fresh idea, while other times I'm left empty-handed as the kernel of inspiration disappears. In those moments, the possibility of a creative consciousness in my immediate present has been nihilated by other, dominant and present concerns.

As a parent at work, I am continuously torn between competing concerns and these include the different versions of myself as an academic, a husband, a son, a friend and a dad. Sartre's 'nothingness' offers a framework to approximate the cohabiting and competing versions of my being as a parent at work. As my conscious self nihilates the possible versions of my future being, so other working parents are forced into similar deviations in their self-construction. The patriarchal organisation is complicit in the inverse nihilation of the caring self on the altar of productivity, and the fictional vessel of the 'ideal worker'.

When thinking about how to write this book, I have caught my consciousness drifting in the 'in-between' of active present, reflective past and speculative future. A fictocriticism is a genre of writing that enables me to explore the existentialism of the blurred identities and 'in-betweenness' of parenthood in paid and unpaid work. A dystopian fictocriticism provides the gifts of a uniquely speculative, imaginative, critical and subversive genre as tools to engage with the embodied, lived experiences, and organisational constraints of parents at work.

DYSTOPIAN FICTOCRITICISM

A dystopian fictocriticism builds upon existing knowledge and writing of fictocriticism in CMOS, which is creative, feminist, critical, genre-bending approach to academic storytelling and research (Brooke, 2002; Gibbs, 1997, 2005; Grafström & Jonsson, 2020; Rhodes, 2015). My approach to this disruptive form of writing is to use dystopian fiction as a uniquely speculative and critical fiction genre (Baccolini & Moylan, 2003; Claeys, 2018) that can simultaneously critique the past and present, while offering a warning to the reader about the possible futures that may await us (Stock, 2016, 2020). In this book, I hope to stir familiar and uncomfortable 'ordinary affects' (Stewart, 2007) that can connect me as a writer with our shared experiences of care and parenthood at work in organisations, at home and the spaced in-between.

While drafting this book, I became a lead carer for my second child, and continued co-parenting my son. My experiences during that time, and my subsequent 'return to work' are entangled and embedded like threads within this text to the extent that the narrative would fall apart if a loose thread was pulled. I initially resisted embracing my full experience of parenthood as part of this writing, but I am grateful to the reviewer of an earlier draft for their permission to push this text into more embodied, reflexive narrative construction. Drawing on these experiences and existing scholarship of 'writing differently' (Beavan, 2020; Fotaki & Harding, 2017; Gilmore et al., 2019; Grafström & Jonsson, 2020; Pullen & Rhodes, 2008; Pullen & Rhodes, 2015; Rhodes, 2009; Rhodes, 2015) I want to emphasise five fluid dimensions (5 Rs) that guide this dystopian fictocriticism of parent at work:

1. **Responsibility** as a writer and researcher of and for parents at work. Including the authorial responsibility to maintain academic rigour, and amplify the argument for radical change.
2. **Relatedness** of the key concepts of organisational fiction and 'fact', masculinity/femininity and care, between parents and my own lived experience, between temporal past, present and future.

3. **Reflexivity** in understanding my authorial role as arbiter of parents' lived experiences alongside my own embodied reflections and speculative relationship with parenthood at work.
4. **Resonance** of my fictocriticism as a version of parenthood at work that offers a shared embodied experiences to evoke affective solidarity.
5. **Resisting** the dominant socio-cultural and structural norms of a patriarchal organisation and academia that privileges a dehumanised, rational masculine experience by creating a community of parents who care.

I will begin with the ethical paradigm of *responsibility* and will address the challenge of academic rigour, respecting the integrity of the participants stories, and authorial intent. Firstly, responsibility pertains to the practice of writing and researching within the field of organisation studies, which is an act of engagement with organisations that are fictional creations and narratives that are fictional interpretations (Rhodes, 2009; Rhodes & Brown, 2005; Savage et al., 2018). To enter into a conceptual dialogue with an organisation is to seek the spaces in-between the people who constitute the essence of the very thing you wish to define. A study of organisations is a study of collective storytelling (Beigi et al., 2019; Gabriel & Connell, 2010; Rhodes, 2001) with the aim to better understand and critique the phenomena that exist within such human social practices. To falsely present empirical findings as in any way objective representations of organisational 'reality' is to mislead and misrepresent the nature of what an organisation is, a story.

This is not to say that a fictocriticism of patriarchal organisations can forgo the need for rigour (Gilmore et al., 2019; Grafström & Jonsson, 2020; Pullen et al., 2020). Researching a topic as emotionally invested and human as parenthood requires a researcher to adopt a high bar for interrelated ethical responsibility (Fotaki & Harding, 2017). This requires close attention to the process of informed consent, data generation, storage, processing, analysis and interpretation. Managing the stories of the participants who contributed to this book (see Appendix 2) required serious reflection on the implications of confidentiality and anonymity through fictionalisation, though I contend participant stories were ethically protected and amplified (Pullen & Rhodes, 2015; Rhodes, 2009). The important amplification occurred through the process of constructing fictional characters that are based upon common traits and themes (see

Appendix 3) derived from critical discourse analysis (Gatto & Callahan, 2021). I also invested in an emotional and ethical responsibility to honour the lived experiences of these parents, something I continue to hold dear beyond the boundaries of this research as my involvement with parents at work continues today.

Rigour is also integral in ensuring that the real-world implications can be realised. At its most impactful, research on the sociological experience of parents at work can address pioneering and comparative parental policy design as part of a coordinated network gender equality (Koslowski et al., 2022; Kvande & Brandth, 2020). The need for rigour when researching and writing about parenthood at work is axiomatic as the people with whom you engage, and for whom you write, *are* often the 'othered' of the patriarchal organisation for whom this research is undertaken.

Recognising the typically detrimental experiences experienced by parents at work, especially in patriarchal organisations (Acker, 1990; Burnett et al., 2012; Correll et al., 2007) emphasises the importance of the ethical authorial responsibility to write in a way that might 'encourage human compassion' (Rhodes, 2009, p. 666). Such noble aspirations can, of course, be subject to bias and misjudgement, but Rhodes proposes that it is the reflexive embracing of the undecidedness of knowledge, and the imperative of the researcher to make decisions about what and how stories are told, that may (as I will discuss shortly) result in resonance with the reader.

This book also adopts a theoretical perspective of critical masculinities, integrating my own ethic of care (Pullen & Rhodes, 2015) within a lens of responsible, caring masculinities (Elliott, 2016; Jordan, 2020; Nelson, 2016). Nelson's (2016) proposal to reinvigorate the concept of 'husbandry' is instructive here as a means of deconstructing the masculine mythology of detachment from 'feminine care' and highlighting the noble acts of careful, attentive, dedicated management. The ethical purpose for a responsible author, as Rhodes outlined, is to resonate with the target audience, not only to encourage compassion, but potentially leading to individual, or collective, acts of allyship and solidarity. Based on this ethical foundation, it is worth considering the fictocriticism form as a vehicle to affect emotion in the reader.

Fictocriticism is probably most readily associated with the *relatedness* of genre and gender, between masculine and feminist academic discourse, and fictional and 'representative' genre narratives. Though strongly affiliated with feminist writing and research (Gibbs, 1997; Jiwa, 2013),

Derrida's (1980) essay on the laws of genre, emphasises the 'madness' or 'othering' of genre and genre as already mixed and 'belonging to one or several genres' (Derrida & Ronell, 1980). This speaks to the 'anti-narrative' intent of the subversive use of fiction in academic writing (De Cock & Land, 2006), which I have drawn on with my use of masculinities theory as an anti-essentialist narrative of parenthood at work. This bending of rules and blurring of boundaries is an individual and collective act of liberation and subversion from the constraint of the genre in CMOS, to elevate the 'poetics of our humanity'(Gilmore et al., 2019, p. 4) beyond the arts and into the canon of academic knowledge. In effect, a fictocriticism can amplify the marginalised voices of those who do not neatly fit inside established academic genre or gender performances.

The relatedness of genre that one might infer from the word 'fictocriticism' could be understood with reference to Derrida's problematisation of 'modes' and 'genres'. For Derrida, a mode does not just exist as a 'linguistic' type such as a 'récit', nor is genre defined purely by its perceived content. Fiction authors of modernist form (such Jocye's deconstruction of narrative form in *Ulysses*) and postmodernist from (such as Atwood's unreliable narrator in the iconic dystopian fiction, *The Handmaid's Tale*) have already laid bare the assumptions of narrative, style, structure and linearity. Yet, the presumed rational, representative 'gold standard' of literary fiction is often promoted in organisational or managerial academic writing on fiction and organisation (see discussions of 'great novels/literature' in Beyes et al., 2019; De Cock & Land, 2006; Michaelson, 2016). The issue, I suggest, with such reverence to 'great' works of fiction, is the predisposition to highlight canonical fiction from the 'greats' who are often men (i.e. Kafka, Dickens, Tolstoy), with fewer examples of canonical women regularly cited, such as Shelley who explored the 'other'. In fact, some women authors have been marginalised by patriarchal publishing biases, such as Budekin's *Swastika Night*, which is arguably a comparable dystopian fiction in its vision to Orwell's Nineteen Eighty-Four (Lothian, 2016; Patai, 1984).

Considering the gendered themes running through storytelling in CMOS writing (Beigi et al., 2019), I have used a genre of fiction that is both peripheral to classically defined 'great literature' as identified in the aforementioned academic discourse, and subversive of the representative (realist fictions) or deductive genres (e.g. detective fictions) that some suggest may help scholars better understand management (Czarniawska-Joerges & De Monthoux, 1994; Kociatkiewicz & Kostera, 2019). I draw upon dystopian fiction as a pioneering, speculative genre that can searingly critique societal problems, while embracing modernist and postmodernist form and style, because it is not bound by conventional genre tropes of chronology and historical context.

My use of relational genre takes heart from Rhodes' (2019) concept of scriptology that opens up possibilities for different modes of writing, such as 'dirty writing' (Pullen & Rhodes, 2008) or 'bad writing' (O'Shea, 2019), that can transcend conventional expectations of the academic mode of writing within the CMOS genre. Importantly, they also construct a separate genre space for embodied experience that enable the othered human voice to be heard. This is where gender relatedness meets genre relatedness to break boundaries (Beavan, 2020; Beavan et al., 2021) where new academic styles generated from lived experience (Boncori & Smith, 2019; O'Shea, 2018) can find an audience and build new knowledge. The knowledge I contribute is related to the masculinities I embody as a parent at work.

I use dialectical relatedness of gender for parents at work, between hegemonic (Connell & Messerschmidt, 2005), caring (Elliott, 2016) and female masculinities (Halberstam, 2019), and the multiple spaces in-between, to construct my own boundary-blurring genre of fictocriticism. I traverse a relatedness of gender through my own embodied fatherhood experiences, which have at times been both conventional and unconventional. I inhabit an uncertain relationship with this identity and it is through reflexivity that I can express my lived experiences.

The importance of **reflexivity** in fictocriticism may be implicitly understood as paramount to an ethical framing of this form of responsible, self-aware writing. Yet self-declarations of positionality, such as my own in this text, open the door to my own authorial privilege in suggesting I can expertly self-analyse my own identity (Rhodes, 2009). **I cannot**. In writing a text that defies convention and opens itself to challenges of rigour, bias and unethical fabrication, it is vital that I state my ongoing undecidedness of how this text can and will be constructed. As a point of note, I wrote the preceding section on relatedness amidst an interruption from my daughter stirring halfway through her nap, which changed the nature of this section and made me compose a short reflection on writing parenthood:

> *Writing parenthood is writing rocking.*
> *It's swaying and soothing, bumping and bopping,*
> *It's cuddling and stroking and thinking about stopping.*

It's searching for signs of sleepiness seeping,
Through stubborn wakefulness, wining and weeping, and
Accepting that daddy does not always know best.

As an author, I do not know best; my privilege is clear to me, but much is unknown of how I am really perceived. This awareness does not, I argue, preclude me from writing about parents at work, rather my consciousness of this *is* a form of 'relational ethics' (Rhodes, 2009) or an 'interrelated organizational ethics' (Fotaki & Harding) as I seek to amplify the 'other' I have encountered. Writing reflexively, in this respect, is an act of opening myself up to constructive art of failure (Callahan & Elliott, 2020; Tienari & Taylor, 2019) in my attempts to ally myself with marginalised parents (mostly women) whose experiences in patriarchal organisations are beyond the scope of my lived experience. My compulsion to write of and for parents at work is an ongoing act of knowledge construction in dialogue with those voices I hope to amplify through resonant storytelling.

The concept of a ***resonant*** fictocriticism is integral to the act of amplifying the voices of the other, especially in the feminist epistemological process of consciousness raising (hooks, 2014). When outlining a polemic for writing differently in CMOS, Grey and Sinclair (2006) argued against the overuse of theory and esoteric academic language as an elitist ticket to a small self-selecting audience. Critical to their argument was the issue of making a difference beyond a small group of scholars 'in the know' by writing more accessible texts that could achieve what I deem to be the core purpose of academia, to generate and communicate new knowledge for the benefit of humanity. Writing a resonant text, I argue, is crucial to achieving this aim.

One feature of fictional writing about working in organisations, as opposed to the 'cleansed', masculine presentation of data within conventionally structured scientific texts (Michaelson, 2016; Pullen & Rhodes, 2008), is to 'complicate and problematise the life of organisations and to raise issues of a moral and social character' (Grafström & Jonsson, 2020, p. 122). Taking the thread of de-cleansing and complication further, I resonate with Beavan's (2020) desire for a 'living scholarship, rich with vibrant colours, where we garden together with our participants, where our sharing work propagates change' (p. 99). The gardener analogy is one that I have always been drawn to as a writer, it resonates because of the process I follow to tend and care (as per husbandry) for the narrative I am constructing, particularly one that benefits from the embodied stories that participants have shared with me.

Resonance comes from writing embodiment; to embrace the lived experience in all its unruly complexity is a worthwhile challenge for a fictocritical text. When done well, such texts endure beyond the immediacy of the key findings, texts like Reinhold's (2018) writing of *becoming animal* and 'the case of the bear' rebound in my consciousness due to their peculiarity and profound emotionality. Reinhold's argument for becoming more intimate with the animal self is highly relevant to the subject of this book. Becoming a parent takes you beyond the consumerist lifestyle and structured, cleansed organisational realities that many have internalised as human subjects in wealthy westernised countries. Though much has been outsourced in family life (and more may follow with the dawn of AI), nothing can approximate the total immersion of that first skin to skin experience with your baby, nor the visceral fear of harm for my wife, Holly during childbirth (Gatto, 2020). The excruciating feeling when your child cries and claws at your arms to hold on as you leave them in nursery never leaves you. These are the scars of embodied, resonant experience that do not fit within conventional organisational writing or life. It is the resistance and subversion of these conventions I turn to in this final section.

Resisting is an active and ongoing process that integrates all of the previous four dimensions. Common across most scholarship of 'writing differently' is the project of feminist subversion of masculine academic conventions to foster 'cooperat[ion] across the spaces that divide us' (Pullen et al., 2020, p. 8). As discussed, this goes beyond the anti-elitist project of aesthetic and accessible writing as outlined by Grey and Sinclair (2006). To write responsibly, reflexively, relatedly and with resonance, the humanising purpose of a fictocriticism should be integral to its narrative.

The subversion of this dystopian fictocriticism, in addition to resisting conventional masculinised writing, is also concerned with subverting the patriarchal culture and structures that devalue care (Bunting, 2020) and actively suppress women in organisations through the 'motherhood penalty' (Brearley, 2021; Correll et al., 2007), which is interrelated with the 'fatherhood forfeit' (Kelland et al., 2022). Such subversive writing is both critical of existing oppression and injustice, while also offering a utopianist counternarrative of hope (Fournier, 2002) and a prefigurative proposal for more inclusive organising by parents, for parents in *our here and now* (Reinecke, 2018).

By adopting a genre that is speculative and critical (Cavalcanti, 2003), I have written an anti-narrative that '[draws] the reader into a creative reconstruction of the past' (Stock, 2016, p. 418). In this book, 'the past' is a temporally fluid concept that considers our immediate past through the lens of future social historians, rendering the 'now' as a historical crisis period akin to 1930s Europe. Doing so, I contend, invites the reader to concentrate their gaze upon the dystopian fiction we are currently inhabiting and co-constructing in our 'here and now', which aligns with the assertion by Savage et al. (2018) that *organisations are fictional creations.* This temporal structure is only possible in a genre that typically aligns with liberal, anti-authoritarian ideology that considers neo-liberal, patriarchal discourse to be exploitative of women and suppressive of caring. The dystopian fictocriticism offers a triad anti-narrative: firstly, it speculates on imaginary ways of living akin to other forms of fiction (De Cock & Land, 2006; Michaelson, 2016); secondly, it warns about the possible futures we may be heading towards, based on the present and past injustices (Atwood, 2017); finally, it offers subversive hope for individual and collective resistance that we, as readers, can take strength from in our daily lives.

To Conclude

These dimensions are not concrete and, though I present them in a notional linear progression from foundation to outcome, they could easily be read in reverse. Even now, as I consciously reflect upon my authorial agenda (Rhodes, 2009) while writing in my present, for my future audience, I accept that I primarily write to resist and resonate. It is, however, my responsibility to critically and reflexively discuss the relatedness of this dystopian fictocriticism, as a transgressive writing that refuses to fit within conventional categories. This book offers a counterhegemonic perspective on some 'dystopian realities' of parents at work; it is an act of resistance that aspires to resonate with the academic reader who may also have been, or is, a parent at work. Throughout the book, I share reconstructed, fictionalised parent stories (from empirical research with 19 parents), alongside my lived experiences in a fabricated organisational context. The point is to disrupt the readers' perception of reality and draw you into the liminal space of fiction where speculative ideas can influence human action.

The difference I offer in this book, compared with other wonderful examples of fictocriticism, is to invert the reader's gaze upon the past, present and future of the organisation as hostile to parents and, by association, women for whom parenthood is an unequally weighted, and unpaid, responsibility. Furthermore, this inverted gaze imagines the nihilated possibilities (Sartre, 2003) of involved, caring masculinities in future speculations of a caring, humane organisation (Korica, 2022; The Care Collective, 2020; Tronto, 2015).

This book is structured in three temporally interrelated acts that follow the narrative device of future gatherings in relation to a fictional present (as seen in the epilogue of *The Handmaid's Tale* by Atwood, 1996). Chapters 2 and 3 are speculative future conference activities that present a critical perspective on parents at work in organisations from the 2020s through archival research methods. The final chapter offers a glimpse into a possible near future and shows the inciting incident that inspires the preceding two chapters, as well as a proposed version of prefigurative organising this book also offers as subversion.

Chapter 2 introduces a parent/academic (an alter ego and autoethnography of my own experiences) who is attending a virtual pre-conference workshop for *the '2130 Societal Family History symposium: concerning the 2029 cloud crash recovery project'*. In this chapter, I attempt to participate in a workshop that reintroduces the method of critical discourse analysis to archival scholars as a means to interrogate archival data fragments using chronologically sensitive methods. In the chapter, one example text is analysed using critical discourse analysis. However, I am constantly distracted by the illnesses of my children.

Chapter 3 is structured as a notional keynote speech at the 2029 centenary of the cloud crash project. This chapter presents the archival data has been reconstructed into the form of a fictional narrative and uses character stories as a basis for thematic discussion (see Appendix 3). I have included two images (Images 3.1 and 3.2) that form the notional cover art for this fictocriticism act as it concerns the organisational experiences in connection to the empirical data that was generated from interviews with 19 participants (see Appendix 2).

I assign gendered pseudonyms to four of the six characters in this narrative to represent the predominantly gendered expectations and experiences I encountered during my interviews. These four characters represent the important chronological aspects of parenthood in patriarchal organisational contexts through expectant and experienced perspectives.

In addition to the four parental amalgam characters, I construct two spectral characters to represent the abstract masculinised 'ghost' organisation, and the collective spirit of 'subversive'. For these characters, I use the collective, gender-neutral pronouns 'they/their' to represent their ethereality. For all my characters, I chose pseudonyms that are primarily inspired by characters in dystopian fiction novels and are indicative of behaviours and attributes associated with their theme.

Chapter 3 is a conversation, inspired by Robin Grenier (2015) and Pullen et al. (2020) and their innovative use of conversation to discuss writing and researching differently. This chapter takes place at an online National Parents and Carers Network meeting during a future 2029 pandemic and offers an embodied, and radical discussion of demands for parents at work that builds on my previous writing (Gatto, 2020).

> *Writing parenthood is writing hope.*
> *It is writing for my children*
> *And writing for new families, yet to form.*
> *It is writing to share and build community,*
> *So a motherhood promise can replace the penalty,*
> *And a fatherhood fraternity can replace the forfeit.*

References

Acker, J. (1990). Hierarchies, jobs, bodies: A theory of gendered organizations. *Gender & Society, 4*(2), 139–158.

Atwood, M. (1996). *The Handmaid's tale* (New ed.). Vintage.

Atwood, M. (2011). Margaret Atwood: The road to Ustopia. *The Guardian.* https://www.theguardian.com/books/2011/oct/14/margaret-atwood-road-to-ustopia

Atwood, M. (2017). Margaret Atwood on what 'the Handmaid's tale' means in the age of Trump. *The New York Times.* https://www.nytimes.com/2017/03/10/books/review/margaret-atwood-handmaids-tale-age-of-trump.html?_r=1

Baccolini, R., & Moylan, T. (2003). Introduction. Dystopia and histories. In R. Baccolini & T. Moylan (Eds.), *Dark horizons: Science fiction and the utopian imagination.* Routledge.

Beavan, K. (2020). Breaking with the masculine reckoning: An open letter to the Critical Management Studies Academy. In A. Pullen, J. Helin, & N. Harding

(Eds.), *Writing differently* (Vol. 4, pp. 91–112). Emerald Publishing Limited. https://doi.org/10.1108/S2046-607220200000004006

Beavan, K., Borgström, B., Helin, J., & Rhodes, C. (2021). Changing writing/ writing for change. *Gender, Work and Organization, 28*(2), 449–455. https://doi.org/10.1111/gwao.12644

Beigi, M., Callahan, J. L., & Michaelson, C. (2019). A critical plot twist: Changing characters and foreshadowing the future of organizational storytelling. *International Journal of Management Reviews, 0*(0). https://doi.org/10.1111/ijmr.12203

Beyes, T., Costas, J., & Ortmann, G. (2019). Novel thought: Towards a literary study of organization. *Organization Studies, 40*(12), 1787–1803. https://doi.org/10.1177/0170840619874458

Boncori, I., & Smith, C. (2019). I lost my baby today: Embodied writing and learning in organizations [Article]. *Management Learning, 50*(1), 74–86. https://doi.org/10.1177/1350507618784555

Brearley, J. (2021). *Pregnant then screwed: The truth about the motherhood penalty and how to fix it.* Simon & Schuster.

Brooke, S. (2002). Does anybody know what happened to "fictocriticism"?: Toward a fractal genealogy of Australian fictocriticism [Other journal article]. *Cultural Studies Review, 8*(2), 104–118. https://doi.org/10.3316/ielapa.200310976

Bunting, M. (2020). *Labours of love: The crisis of care.* Granta Books.

Burnett, S., Gatrell, C., Cooper, C., & Sparrow, P. (2012). Fathers at work: A ghost in the organizational machine. *Gender, Work and Organization, 20*(6). https://doi.org/10.1111/gwao.12000

Callahan, J. L., & Elliott, C. (2020). Fantasy spaces and emotional derailment: Reflections on failure in academic activism. *Organization, 27*(3), 506–514. https://doi.org/10.1177/1350508419831925

Cavalcanti, I. (2003). The writing of Utopia and the feminist critical dystopia. In R. Baccolini & T. Moylan (Eds.), *Dark horizons: Science fiction and the dystopian imagination.* Routledge.

Claeys, G. (2018). *Dystopia: A natural history.* Oxford University Press.

Connell, R. (2005). A really good husband – Work/life balance, gender equity and social change [Article]. *Australian Journal of Social Issues, 40*(3), 369–383. https://doi.org/10.1002/j.1839-4655.2005.tb00978.x

Connell, R., & Messerschmidt, J. W. (2005). Hegemonic masculinity: Rethinking the concept. *Gender & Society, 19*(6), 829–859.

Correll, S. J., Benard, S., & Paik, I. (2007). Getting a job: Is there a motherhood penalty? *American Journal of Sociology, 112*(5), 1297–1338.

Czarniawska-Joerges, B., & De Monthoux, P. (1994). *Good novels, better management: Reading organizational realities in fiction.* Routledge.

De Cock, C., & Land, C. (2006). Organization/literature: Exploring the seam. *Organization Studies, 27*(4), 517–535.

Derrida, J., & Ronell, A. (1980). The law of Genre. *Critical Inquiry, 7*(1), 55–81. http://www.jstor.org/stable/1343176

Elliott, K. (2016). Caring masculinities:Theorizing an emerging concept. *Men and Masculinities, 19*(3), 240–259. https://doi.org/10.1177/1097184x15576203

Federici, S. (2021). *Patriarchy of the wage: Notes on Marx, gender, and feminism.* PM Press.

Fotaki, M., & Harding, N. (2017). Feminist ethics as nomadic minoritarianism and relational embodiment in organizations. In M. Fotaki & N. Harding (Eds.), *Gender and the organization: Women at work in the 21st century.* Routledge.

Fournier, V. (2002). Utopianism and the cultivation of possibilities: Grassroots movements of hope. *The Sociological Review, 50*(1_suppl), 189–216.

Gabriel, Y., & Connell, N. A. D. (2010). Co-creating stories: Collaborative experiments in storytelling. *Management Learning, 41*(5), 507–523. https://doi.org/10.1177/1350507609358158

Gatto, M. (2020). Parenthood demands: Resisting a dystopia in the workplace. *Human Resource Development International, 23*(5), 569–585. https://doi.org/10.1080/13678868.2020.1735832

Gatto, M., & Callahan, J. (2021). Exposing interpellation with dystopian fiction: A critical discourse analysis technique to disrupt hegemonic masculinity. In V. Stead, C. Elliot, & S. Mavin (Eds.), *Handbook of research methods on gender and management.* Edward Elgar Publishing.

Gibbs, A. (1997). Bodies of words: Feminism and fictocriticism – Explanation and demonstration. *Text, 1*(2) https://doi.org/http://www.textjournal.com.au/oct97/gibbs.htm

Gibbs, A. (2005). Fictocriticism, affect, mimesis: Engendering differences. *Text, 9*(1) http://www.textjournal.com.au/april05/gibbs.htm

Gilmore, S., Harding, N., Helin, J., & Pullen, A. (2019). Writing differently. *Management Learning, 50*(1), 3–10. https://doi.org/10.1177/1350507618811027

Grafström, M., & Jonsson, A. (2020). When fiction meets theory: Writing with voice, resonance, and an open end. In A. Pullen, J. Helin, & N. Harding (Eds.), *Writing differently* (Vol. 4, pp. 113–129). Emerald Publishing Limited. https://doi.org/10.1108/S2046-607220200000004007

Grenier, R. S. (2015). Autoethnography as a legitimate approach to HRD research: A methodological conversation at 30,000 feet. *Human Resource Development Review, 14*(3), 332–350.

Grey, C., & Sinclair, A. (2006). Writing differently. *Organization, 13*(3), 443–453. https://doi.org/10.1177/1350508406063492

Halberstam, J. (2019). *Female masculinity.* Duke University Press.

Hochschild, A. R. (1979). Emotion work, feeling rules, and social structure. *American Journal of Sociology, 85*(3), 551–575. https://doi.org/10.1086/227049

hooks, b. (2014). *Feminism is for everybody : Passionate politics: Passionate politics.* Taylor & Francis Group. http://ebookcentral.proquest.com/lib/northumbria/detail.action?docID=1813118

Jiwa, F. (2013). Beyond autoethnography: Fictocriticism as a feminist writing strategy. *South Asian Review, 34*(3), 103–120. https://doi.org/10.1080/02759527.2013.11932943

Jordan, A. (2020). Masculinizing care? Gender, ethics of care, and fathers' rights groups. *Men and Masculinities, 23*(1), 20–41. https://doi.org/10.1177/1097184x18776364

Kelland, J., Lewis, D., & Fisher, V. (2022). Viewed with suspicion, considered idle and mocked-working caregiving fathers and fatherhood forfeits. *Gender, Work and Organization, n/a*(n/a). https://doi.org/10.1111/gwao.12850

Kociatkiewicz, J., & Kostera, M. (2019). The body in the library: An investigative celebration of deviation, hesitation, and lack of closure. *Management Learning, 50*(1), 114–128. https://doi.org/10.1177/1350507618780367

Korica, M. (2022). A hopeful manifesto for a more humane academia. *Organization Studies, 0*(0), 01708406221106316. https://doi.org/10.1177/01708406221106316

Koslowski, A., Blum, S., Dobrotić, I., Kaufman, G., & Moss, P. (2022). International review of leave policies and research 2022. http://www.leavenetwork.org/lp_and_r_reports/.

Kvande, E., & Brandth, B. (2020). Designing parental leave for fathers – Promoting gender equality in working life. *International Journal of Sociology and Social Policy, 40*(5/6), 465–477. https://doi.org/10.1108/IJSSP-05-2019-0098

Lothian, A. (2016). A speculative history of no future: Feminist negativity and the queer dystopian impulses of Katharine Burdekin's swastika night. *Poetics Today, 37*(3), 443–472.

Michaelson, C. (2016). A novel approach to business ethics education: Exploring how to live and work in the 21st century. *Academy of Management Learning & Education, 15*(3), 588–606.

Nelson, J. A. (2016). Husbandry: A (feminist) reclamation of masculine responsibility for care. *Cambridge Journal of Economics, 40*(1), 1–15.

O'Shea, S. C. (2018). This girl's life: An autoethnography. *Organization, 25*(1), 3–20. https://doi.org/10.1177/1350508417703471

O'Shea, S. C. (2019). My dysphoria blues: Or why I cannot write an autoethnography. *Management Learning, 50*(1), 38–49. https://doi.org/10.1177/1350507618791115

Patai, D. (1984). *Orwell's despair, Burdekin's hope: Gender and power in dystopia.* Women's Studies International Forum.

Pullen, A., & Rhodes, C. (2008). Dirty writing. *Culture and Organization, 14*(3), 241–259. https://doi.org/10.1080/14759550802270684

Pullen, A., & Rhodes, C. (2015). Ethics, embodiment and organizations. *Organization, 22*(2), 159–165. https://doi.org/10.1177/1350508414558727

Pullen, A., Helin, J., & Harding, N. (2020). *Writing differently*. Emerald Group Publishing.

Reinecke, J. (2018). Social movements and prefigurative organizing: Confronting entrenched inequalities in occupy London. *Organization Studies, 39*(9), 1299–1321. https://doi.org/10.1177/0170840618759815

Reinhold, E. (2018). How to become animal through writing: The case of the bear. *Culture and Organization, 24*(4), 318–329.

Rhodes, C. (2001). *Writing organization: (Re)presentation and control in narratives at work*. John Benjamins. https://www.jbe-platform.com/content/books/9789027298362

Rhodes, C. (2009). After reflexivity: Ethics, freedom and the writing of organization studies. *Organization Studies, 30*(6), 653–672. https://doi.org/10.1177/0170840609104804

Rhodes, C. (2015). Writing organization/romancing fictocriticism. *Culture and Organization, 21*(4), 289–303.

Rhodes, C. (2019). Sense-ational organization theory! Practices of democratic scriptology. *Management Learning, 50*(1), 24–37. https://doi.org/10.1177/1350507618800716

Rhodes, C., & Brown, A. D. (2005). Writing responsibly: Narrative fiction and organization studies. *Organization, 12*(4), 467–491.

Sartre, J.-P. (2003). *Being and nothingness: An essay on phenomenological ontology*. Routledge.

Savage, P., Cornelissen, J. P., & Franck, H. (2018). Fiction and organization studies. *Organization Studies, 39*(7), 975–994.

Stewart, K. (2007). *Ordinary affects*. Duke University Press. https://books.google.co.uk/books?id=A3pKPTPWC3AC

Stock, A. (2016). The future-as-past in dystopian fiction [conceptual]. *Poetics Today, 37*(3), 415–442. https://doi.org/10.1215/03335372-3599495

Stock, A. (2020). *Modern dystopian fiction and political thought: Narratives of world politics*. Routledge.

The Care Collective. (2020). *The care manifesto: The politics of interdependence*. Verso.

Tienari, J., & Taylor, S. (2019). Feminism and men: Ambivalent space for acting up. *Organization, 26*(6), 948–960. https://doi.org/10.1177/1350508418805287

Tronto, J. C. (2015). *Who cares? How to reshape a democratic politics* (1st ed.). Cornell University Press. https://doi.org/10.7591/j.ctt18kr598

CHAPTER 2

Pre-conference Workshop 2130

Abstract This fictocritical chapter introduces the autoethnographic and methodological elements of this dystopian fictocriticism in the form of a narrator attending a future virtual pre-conference workshop. The chapter adopts a fusion of fiction, autobiography and critical discourse analysis to describe how the gender inequity for parents at work can be researched differently. The purpose of this chapter is to introduce the lived experience of parenthood and subvert prevailing masculinised academic research methods and writing.

Keywords Parents • Work • Organisations • Critical discourse analysis • Patriarchy

PRE-CONFERENCE WORKSHOP

Welcome, colleagues! We will wait a few moments for all your avatars to fully manifest, I know some of you have made last minute aesthetic changes. Once we are all together, we can begin our journey, upriver! While you are waiting, please take a look…

The silky voice of this tall, imposing, green alien figure floats through the synthetic air and echoes around my oversized VR headset. It is distorting the whimpering, escalating cries from my daughter, Abbie, fussing downstairs with her mummy, Debbie. I arch my back as the Alien avatar

M. Gatto, *Parents at Work*, https://doi.org/10.1007/978-3-031-15482-9_2

greeter continues their warm welcome and I switch frequencies to focus more on my daughter's cry. It's her distress cry, the same one she had during the night when I woke at 2 and 4am, before her 5.30 full wake. I'm onto my fourth coffee today; it's slowly going tepid in my flask mug, so I press the reheat function and wait the ponderous 30 seconds before I can sip something hot again.

Abbie's distress is rapidly becoming anger and frustration and I briefly type a holding message *'be right back'*, in the workshop chat room, but don't send. I lift my headset and check my watch; it's 9.55. She can have some paracetamol soon. I put the headset back on to double check that the Alien is still rambling on. There are a growing number of fellow avatars materialising around me. Many have also gone green this year, I must have missed the memo as my all-grey wizard robes are standing out like a sore thumb. The VR environment is garish, too. Bright pink and orange flora are scattered across rolling hills, glowing and pulsating with disconcerting regularity, just as nature intended. I assume it's some neo-modernist theory of creativity and engagement, but it's also an assault on my weary eyes. What I wouldn't give for beige right now.

I stand on the banks of a river and a Viking-style longship is moored at end of a grand, oak jetty. A row of oars juts out of its wooden hull, their paddles lapping against the gentle tide. 'They're going to make us row, aren't they?' A withering voice asks from behind my field of vision. I turn and see a woman in a white and black astronaut suit, her visor is down and she is stony faced.

'I guess so.' I reply, feigning a wry smile.

'Good thing my VR kit is not set up for resistance training.' She says with a small chuckle. 'My post pregnancy body can't cope with this kind of excursion.'

'Oh, how are you doing? How is your baby? My name's Nick, by the way.'

'Roxy. I'm fine thanks, baby's doing fine. My mum's here so I can attend this.'

'I see you didn't get the memo, too.' I say, gesturing to my robes and smiling.

'No, I got it. I don't wear green, and I always wanted to be an astronaut, so here I am.' She smiles and flicks her visor into place. We both laugh and I turn back to the longship.

'What do you think?'

'The boat?'

'Yeah'

'It's probably some crude metaphor to incapsulate the journey we are about the go on together, and the whole *past, present and future* thing.'

'Hah! This is clearly not your first pre-conference workshop!' Roxy states with a sarcastic tone.

'Indeed it is not. Furthermore, I predict that our future will be a shared endeavour and the learning we explore together will be heutagogical.'

'Ah, that's where you're wrong! I've seen the course notes, we're in for a more didactic experience today.'

'How did you get access to the notes?'

'I'm one of the facilitators for this session.' Roxy replies with a smile.

'I see...' I weigh up my options before letting out an embarrassed laugh.

'Anyway, I have to have a quick chat with Gibson before we disembark. It's been good to chat to a fellow fashion pioneer. I love the robes, very Gandalf!'

'Likewise. I'll be with you shortly, I have a crying baby downstairs and I'd better go and help before I start limbering up for the rowing.'

Roxy takes long bounding steps towards Gibson floating momentarily in the low gravity atmosphere. I lament my VR set's limited functionality and make a mental note to run an update as my platform judders due to EMP interference from my mug. The buzzer alarm continues to indicate optimal temperature has been achieved so I switch off the heater and take a deep slug of the reheated coffee+. Fast-acting caffeine hits me instantaneously and I roll my aching shoulders to jolt my body into action.

A message appears on my feed, marked priority. I twitch my left index finger to display the text:

> Please can you come downstairs to help me for a minute, she's just been sick all over me and there's a poonami.

Dropping my headset on my desk, I rush out of the room and cascade downstairs. Dodging the pile of washing on the mid-landing step, I am hit by the cacophony of crying that bounces around our hallway.

I step, tentatively into the lounge and am hit by the familiar smell of acetone. Debbie is on her knees in the middle of a nappy change, thick yellow vomit is painted down her sleeve. I look down to Abbie and notice her nappy rash has flared up bright red, too. She's writhing on the floor and I kneel down beside her and hold her torso on the mat to get her cleaned up.

'Go and get a change of clothes' I say to Debbie and she hauls herself upright to head upstairs.

It feels wrong to restrain Abbie like this, it's one of the aspects of parenthood we don't tend to share, but it's this or chase her around the room while she smears poo everywhere. That would make for a unique VR environment! I wipe the poo away quickly, I've had plenty of practice and it's second nature now. I find a crumpled set of spare clothes in the changing pile and commence the task of further irritating Abbie. By the end, she is furious and directing her crying at me with tears streaming down her face. I lift her up and cuddle her the moment she is dressed. Taking her into the hall, I find the mirror and point to Abbie and myself in the glass. She pauses her cry and looks at the doppelgangers staring back at us. I often wonder what it is Abbie thinks she is looking at. Does she realise or does she long to interact with the little baby behind the glass? In these moments, time slows down, I can feel the weight of her body against my left hip and enjoy our connection.

Debbie returns from downstairs. She has changed her outfit and looks flushed.

'How long is your course on for, today?' She asks.

'It's four hours, but we have a 45 minute break in the middle. Let's have lunch then. Can I get you anything now? Oh, we should give her paracetamol now.'

'Yes, please can you get it?'

I run upstairs to collect the bottle of suspension paracetamol from our medicine cabinet. I look outside to the backyard. The rain has been pouring for two straight days and a large puddle has formed that is creeping towards our back door. We have flood barriers up permanently these days, but there is something innately stressful about watching water slowly ooze towards you. I take a syringe and measure 5mls before running back downstairs.

I leave Abbie with Debbie and take a lingering glance as Abbie attempts to follow me out of the room. It is a jarring experience to leave her, but the boat is probably about to disembark and I don't fancy a VR swim to catch it up. I get back to my desk and pick up the headset. Plunging back into the VR world, I re-occupy my avatar and almost loose balance as the auto-pilot has taken me to the brink of the longship hull. Beneath my feet, a gurgling silvery soup bubbles and like primordial liquid teaming with microbes. As I step onto the deck, Gibson, the lead workshop facilitator, greets me with a smile and hands me a horn filled with what he describes as 'synthetic, alcohol-free mead'. My taste buds are almost exploding in anticipation.

Gibson steps to the helm of the boat and begins his introductory announcement.

'My fellow scholars! I am Professor Gibson Morgan and this is my colleague is Dr Roxy Butler. Welcome to our voyage into the past!'

Roxy stands next to Gibson on an elevated wooden platform at the keel. Behind them the back of a dragon's head points downriver. Gibson begins to speak.

> We have chosen an iconic vessel for this journey, one that struck fear into the hearts of indigenous coastal communities. Our purpose today is not to engender fear, but we do plan to invade the data archive of the pre-pandemic epoch that we have finally been granted access to following the unanticipated success of last year's centenary keynote. This is our chance to explore stories from over 100 years ago. Stories that have shaped our current reality, and the ancestral experiences that echo through time. Roxy and I have spent considerable time contemplating the most appropriate tools to investigate this treasure trove and we alighted on a now chronically underused methodological technique called Critical Discourse Analysis (Fairclough, 2013). In today's workshop we will be co-constructing an archival approach to a method that Dr Butler and I have feel can bring fresh perspectives to our shared understanding of Societal Family History, and gender relations at work. Importantly, and in light of rising contemporary unrest emerging from the neo-manosphere, we are drawing on chronologically sensitive references (White, 2040) that can immerse us in the scholarship of that time period. This will be a comprehensive journey into our past to help us better understand the possible futures we are heading towards. For now, let us raise a horn to researching family sociology and our shared mission to expand our collective knowledge of its rich and tumultuous history.

Gibson lifts his ornately carved wood-effect horn into the sky and a bejewelled helmet appears on his head. There is a murmur of laughter as we observe similar helmets flash into existent atop our heads too, especially as some have become embedded in people's alien avatar heads, but the chuckles turn to sighs as the long oars appear adjacent to our allocated seats. Immersive VR is sometimes too immersive.

The journey to our workshop environment is uneventful and I take the opportunity to engage autopilot again so I can check in with Debbie. I re-enter reality and hear winging from downstairs. Before I head down, I do a sweep of my son's room to tidy up the immediate mess. I wince as I tread on a toy car carefully placed next to a pile of cushions by to the doorway. Picking it up, I'm torn between frustration at the untidiness and a carefree acceptance of the ridiculousness of my homelife at times. I gather up the cushions and throw them back on his bed before scooping up some dirty clothes and exiting the room to head downstairs. The winging rings in my ears and I consciously try to push it into background noise. I pop my head into the room when Debbie and Abbie are entwined in a swaying hold. Abbie looks exhausted, her cheeks are still flushed and her eyes are lolling between wakefulness and sleep. Debbie pleads at me to take her and I step forward to accept the transfer.

'I'm desperate for the loo and need to drink.' Debbie whispers.

I nod and take hold of Abbie whose crying escalates while she glares at Debbie.

'Why won't she settle on me?' Debbie says.

'She smells your milk. Go on, I'll get her to sleep.' I say as Debbie heads out of the room and I begin rocking Abbie. She continues crying and begins rubbing her head on my chest. A smear of stringy, sticky, light green mucus decorates my t-shirt. I increase the depth of my sway, dipping my legs and feeling the familiar strain on my back and shoulder is flaring up, too. Her head presses into the soft tissue above my collar bone as I establish the dipping rhythm. Dare I ease off and establish a shallow dip? My thighs are imploring me to stop...

* * *

PRESENT DAY—MARCH 24TH 2023
It's 13.55 and I'm mentally preparing myself to begin writing this section of the chapter when I feel a buzzing emanating from my phone. I pull out my phone and see the identification label I always dread 'Nursery'. My heart sinks and I press the answer button to begin the call. I retain a glimmer of hope, based on recent nursery calls I have received that were innocuous, such as permission to go on an impromptu outing. As Ailish says hello, I beg her to follow up with 'there's nothing to worry about', or words to that effect. In the past, when I have heard such reassurances, I feel elated, as if I have received a stay of execution. Not today.

'I'm calling to say that unfortunately Sara has had a large vomit about 15 minutes ago, followed by another one as she was being changed.

'Oh no.' To my shame, I don't even think to ask if she is currently OK.

'Yeah, I know. She's had a really bad run, but at least she made it through to Thursday this week.'

This is absolutely not a consolation for me, but I agree out of politeness, 'Yes, that's true.' I wait for the inevitable reality that is about to crush my plans.

'I'm afraid we need you to come to pick her up and she will have to be off for 48 hours.'

There it is.

'Of course. Thank you for letting me know. I'm on my way.'

As I prepare to leave, I weigh up the positives and negatives of also collecting my Leo. He's in pre-school now and was fine this morning. Will it be easier to get them both now? Helena is at work so it's down to me. I decide that I need to prioritise Sara and cross the bridge of the second pick-up when it arrives in three hours' time.

It's a short drive to the nursery, I call me mum to vent at the most recent in the series of illnesses that have befallen us. She is also ill with COVID-19, alongside my dad. I spoke to her earlier and know she is feeling lousy, but OK, yet I still take pause to worry when I hear her coughing down the phone. I thank her for listening to my moan and I spend the rest of the journey reflecting on what it means to be a parent at work, especially for this book and the concept of 'dirty writing' (Pullen & Rhodes, 2008). Should I cleanse this experience from my carefully constructed dystopian fiction, or should I, like Boncori and Smith (2019), embrace my imperfect, embodied experience of parenthood at work and in writing? I manage to find a parking space in the crowded carpark. I enter the building and hear the sound of young children on the stairs. I immediately confront the possibility of my son seeing me and the confusion this could cause. I'm embarrassed to say that I ducked inside the door frame to the baby room, hastily kicked of my shoes and slunk into the room. I even felt the acute sense of achievement at my dynamic dad manoeuvre, which I'm sure looked truly pathetic to any bystander.

As I recompose myself, I see Sara is standing holding some soft play furniture. She looks happy and smiles when she sees me. I'm not going to lie, the thought crossed my mind 'why am I here?' However, in such moments I am reminded of the essential relatedness of parenthood and an interdependence with those people who also care for and educate my children. My parental '*dependence on those others makes relationality an essential precondition of [my] own survival*' (Fotaki & Harding, 2017,

p. 144). I resolve to trust the relationship and proceed to collect the sluiced clothes from Sara's basket. I pick her up, and kiss her on the forehead, just as I did five hours ago at drop off before she waved goodbye to me.

Walking to the car, I notice that Sara is looking a little pale. I hope the 'fresh' roadside air might be a relief. She is fairly happy to be placed in the car and I play peekaboo as I fail to properly close her door twice.

Driving home is going fine until I notice she has had a small vomit that is dribbling down her chin. She starts to cry. Then a larger vomit comes. I am stuck on a main road, just before a roundabout. Home is less than five minutes away. She vomits again and my heart pounds as I notice her gasping for breath. I look in my rear mirror and frantically seek a possible place to pull over.

She starts to cry again and I breathe. This is one of the most welcome cries I have heard in months. I commence my reassuring narrative that we are nearly home and continuously apologise that she is going through this. She vomits again. Her top is soaked with yellow and light brown chunky vomit (apologies, this colour description may be inaccurate, I am colourblind).

Writing Parenthood is Writing Illness.
It is writing about cleaning up sick
from grey car seat fabric with a baby wipe,
Rubbing the smeared chunks and clumping them
Into a ball while my stomach churns.
It is snatching moments to reflect,
while my son asks me questions.
It is loading the washing machine with my daughter on my hip,
And watching the cycle begin.
It is a process of cleaning, comforting and caring.

Embodied, compromised caring: a voice note

I am now sat with my daughter on my lap. She has recently vomited, multiple times in the car and in the nursery. I'm feeling guilty for recording this voice note while she is upset and I'm hoping that the distraction of Mr Tumble on TV will provide me the opportunity to share my immediate embodied experience. Being a parent at work breaks down the boundaries of paid and unpaid work of care, of disembodied experiences where I internalized the pressure of work deadlines and compromise my carer duties as a parent. Writing this book is a testament to the almost intolerable tension between paid work and unpaid and care. Listening to my daughter cry is horrible. Feeling her twist and writhe as I record this note is a moral injury I am doing to myself. My only ethical justification is that I do so in service of other parents, many of whom experience far worse and do not have the space or resources to express their anguish by using their voice. Being a parent at work is a constant battle with insufficient time and energy, and results in a moral injury that is subsumed within our fragmented paid and unpaid work selves.

*   *   *

Pre-conference Workshop—2130
We disembark the long ship and enter a large banquet hall through a simple oak door that is unceremoniously cut out within a grand, far larger oak door. This level of nuanced detail in a VR environment is baffling to me, but evokes warm memories of a cathedral I used to visit years ago, before the flood.

A long, dark, walnut table dissects the room and strewn across the surface are cuttings of printed data. It is quaint to see simulation, weathered paper. I remember by grandparents talking about using colouring crayons on sheet after sheet of paper when they were little and recoiling at the waste.

I wander over to the first scrap of paper, reach out my hand and touch the surface. It's smooth, yet mottled, like the sunburnt skin on my arm. I use my VR focus function to centre the data sample and generate a notes field around it. I start reading the words on the page, it's like stepping into someone's head, uninvited, but there is something compelling here. I try to shake the feeling of exploitation, as if I am as bad as the Egyptologists who excavated mummies and removed their sarcophaguses, before displaying in museums for millions of people to view. This feels wrong, but then I remind myself of the value of their story, and their consent to share it. It feels like a fine line. Did they consent to THIS? Do any participants knowingly consent to the exact treatment of their stories when analysed, interpreted and weaved into a narrative?

I stare at the fabricated paper and feel irritated as the fakery that attempts to evoke mirth in us as delegates. I read it again. Is there something good that can come out of this? Can I stretch the boundaries of moral relativism? I start to read it for a third time when I feel the unmistakable buzzing of meta-collaborate alert. I drown in apathy when I see it is from Gibson.

'*Delegates, please join me with Nick to participate in some live critical discourse analysis.*' His voice echoes and rasps as if announced through a dusty tannoy.

I feel the billowing of buzzes as the delegates enter my meta viewpoint and sit, unseen and passive, behind my shoulder. I've always hated these live collaboration sessions.

'*This is what scholars from the pre-pandemic used to call a teachable moment*' Gibson begins. '*Roxy and I had hoped one of you would **take the plunge** so to speak, and use your intuition to seek a story you connect with. Most of you have glanced at some of the parchments, but Nick here has been staring at this one for five minutes. Tell us, Nick, what has resonated with you?*'

Oh, spare me, please! This must be what my son feels like when I coax him into the educational VR worldbuilder game we lovingly selected for his birthday, when all he really wants to do is ride the mastodon through the Martian mountain ranges, like his friends.

'*Well...*' I pause for effect, projecting an aura of reflective contemplation, while I search for adequate words to mask my ignorance. '*What struck me when reading this is the internalised patriarchal attitudes that she's sharing.*' I hear a hum of approval from behind me, it's always a winner to use the 'P' word with societal family history audiences. With growing confidence, I take a breath to speak again, but am clipped by Gibson's larger preparatory inhalation that rushes around my right ear.

'*Excellent, Nick. You have alighted at our principal protagonist in the process of critical discourse analysis, ideology.*'

'*What does patriarchy have to do with ideology.*' Another voice enters the fray.

Gibson excitedly reorientates the meta-space and projects his minimised avatar onto the sample page. He is now holding a tall battle-axe and uses it to swipe at the words alongside him. It is a comical scene, and a few delegates join me in a snort of incredulity. That being said, I feel myself being swept up in his passion, energy and commitment to the role. It's an engaging approach, I'll give him that.

'*Roxy, please join me on the parchment.*' Gibson calls out and is instantly joined by her astronaut avatar. '*Please share with the group our theoretical lens for this exercise in critical discourse analysis.*'

A miniaturised Roxy appears in the top right of the parchment and lowers her reflective visor. The sliding noise ends with a satisfying click and she smiles before taking a deep breath.

Roxy begins, her voice is clear and authoritative, '*Thanks Gibson. Many of you will be familiar with modern day patriarchy, but we are interested in its role in the pre-pandemic epoch for parents within organisations. Patriarchy is a reproduced ideology of masculine privilege that functions through the oppression of women. By viewing this artefact as a text example of parental discourse, we can look for the presence of patriarchy in her words as evidence of a parent's interpellation[1] to patriarchy. What Gibson and I are putting to you as researchers, is that this parent and the others on this table are, to varying degrees, subjects and co-constructors of patriarchy. What these subjects say can be coded for markers of patriarchy at different levels of social integration. The reproduction can be at a micro individual level, meso relational level, or macro ideological level. The interpellation of these subjects ensures the survival and enduring domination of the patriarchal social discourse. Through reading these text artifacts, we can identify social events and practices that subjectify parents (mostly women) as subjugated to the hierarchical power of men.*'

There is a long pause in the room as the delegates in the meta-space hush their breathing. Gibson stands proudly, holding a long battle axe and lifts it up in the air.

'*Roxy and I are going to demonstrate this for you with this text.*' As Gibson speaks, he lifts his battle-axe to point to the first section of the text. The phrase '*hunter gatherer*' becomes bold. Roxy makes a comic gesture of lifting her visor before she fires up her jet pack to fly over to the other side of the page. A flume of white dust follows her across the text and dissipates

---

[1] Interpellation, as coined by Louis Althusser, is the process whereby ideological ideas are internalised and reproduced by individuals. 'Concrete individuals' are hailed as 'concrete subjects' of dominant systems (such as patriarchy) and are described as 'always already' subjects of the ideological norms of society. Through the workplace rituals and social norms affiliated with parenthood, individuals are 'hailed' as subjects to participate in the reproduction of these norms. For example, when an expectant father is invited by a colleague to discuss their career prospects and encouraged to assume their responsibility as a 'breadwinner', their acceptance of this conversation and conformity with this expectation illustrates interpellation to patriarchal discourse and serves to reproduce patriarchal norms

as she lands on the other side. She generates a speech bubble and begins populating the analysis comment. I feel the familiar buzzing in my headset and a private message appears across my screen:

THE NURSERY CALLED, LEO'S BEEN SICK. WE NEED TO GO TO GET HIM.

My fears are realised. I think back to the drop-off this morning and the comments I dismissed.

'Daddy, my tummy feels sore'.

'I know, but I'm sure it will improve as the day goes on.' I said, reassuring myself more than I expect I am reassuring him. We were greeted by the *Mary24* welcome-bot who did the customary temperature sweep before admitting entrance. I stayed quiet and put on my broadest smile as we were admitted to the hybrid play space. I observed the Virtual educators calling out to their VR children to stay close and respect the temples. The board said they are exploring Durbar Square in Kathmandu today, presumably without the sim worshippers. I guided Leo to his educator, Connie. We pay a premium for him to experience the real deal, including daily outing to their walled, solar insulated garden. I could also smell the breakfast snack that's on its way, buttered toast. Some things never change.

On our drive home, Leo is drifting off to sleep. I call ahead to Debbie and ask if it's ok for me to get him down for a nap and resume the course. She agrees and I rush through the naptime ritual, ensuring a sick-bowl is placed by his bed. I can smell sulphur on his breath and start feeling the familiar twinges, I hope in sympathy, emanating from my own tummy. Once settled, I nip back to my VR headset and resume the session. It's silent on the screen and I realise it's the scheduled 45 minute break, which is imperfect timing given my window for participation is rapidly diminished. My meta collaboration space remains intact and I look at the frozen image (see Fig. 2.1).

Writing Parenthood is Writing Interruptions.
It's writing in the spaces in between care,
While worrying about your son's poorly tummy.
Or, thinking about an introductory line, while he asks
A question about the structure we are driving past.
It's stopping to appreciate his curiosity and wonder,
And embracing the tangential thought amidst

Masculinities in Working Parent Discourses

	Oryx - ...although he's [Crake] keen to be involved he of	Macro discourse of patriarchal breadwinner.

Oryx - ...although he's [Crake] keen to be involved he of
hunter gatherer **instinct**, male instinct with, there is
some of that, where, you know, **he wants to provide for**
the family he wants to be the **batman** who does that. you
know. you know he's a **very male, male** and that's. that's
fine and **I've gone with that**. Not because I believe in
that, not necessarily, but because I **understand the**
nature, human nature, but I also from the financial
point of view it makes more sense.

Mark: Sure, sure. That's absolutely fine.

Oryx: **Whether that's to my detriment or not it might be**
career wise. We try not to let it be [pause] it depends on
your support network as well.

Macro discourse of patriarchal breadwinner.

Figurative evocation of vigilante, protective masculine role as father.

Micro discourse of internalised maternal role

Macro discourse of essentialism in perception of roles.

Meso discourse of economic constraint on gender equality for parents.

Meso discourse of relational awareness of the motherhood penalty.

Meso discourse of relational interdependency of parenthood at work.

Fig. 2.1 Critical discourse text example

The perception of order and beautiful disorder.

I head downstairs to help with Debbie's lunch. Abbie is on pureed food and water. We heat up the leftovers from last night's tofu curry and sit together while Abbie wipes her eyes in my lap. Debbie looks totally shattered. I feel the guilt rising in me and search for any words that can make the situation better.

'How long is left in the workshop?' She asks in a low voice.

'Two hours, with a fifteen minute break in between.'

As the 45-minute break draws to a close, I hear the inevitable sound of Leo calling for me. It was so much easier at last year's conference when Debbie was pregnant.

REFERENCES

Boncori, I., & Smith, C. (2019). I lost my baby today: Embodied writing and learning in organizations [Article]. *Management Learning, 50*(1), 74–86. https://doi.org/10.1177/1350507618784555

Fairclough, N. (2013). *Critical discourse analysis: The critical study of language.* Routledge.

Fotaki, M., & Harding, N. (2017). Feminist ethics as nomadic minoritarianism and relational embodiment in organizations. In M. Fotaki & N. Harding (Eds.), *Gender and the organization: Women at work in the 21st century.* Routledge.

Pullen, A., & Rhodes, C. (2008). Dirty writing. *Culture and Organization, 14*(3), 241–259. https://doi.org/10.1080/14759550802270684

White, R. (2040). Chronology sensitive referencing: An archival methodology for historical scholarship. *Fictional Journal of Archival Research Methods, 60*(3), 232–252.

CHAPTER 3

Dystopian Fictocriticism

Abstract I present this fictocriticism as a 'genre-bending' (Rhodes, *Culture and Organization* 21:289–303, 2015, p. 294) dystopian fiction and interpretation of the empirical data, as discussed in the previous chapter. I follow an archival structural approach to this narrative, akin to existing character-led dystopian fictions (*see The Testaments, The Power, and Red Clocks)*, to construct my own character-led dystopian fiction. Utilising two images to 'bookend' the chapter as empirical, my dystopian fictocriticism depicts six characters who embody aspects of the 19 participants I interviewed. These six characters are fictional creations, combining attributes, experiences and themes that arose during the interviews and analysis. I construct complex characters who are faithful representations of the sometimes-contradictory range of expectations and experiences of the parents I interviewed.

Keywords Dystopian fictocriticism • Patriarchy • Subversion • Masculinities

> **Writing parents at work, is writing fear**
> Of the present and fear of the futures.
> It's failing to take my eyes away from the
> Horror of political posturing and

© The Author(s), under exclusive license to Springer Nature
Switzerland AG 2023
M. Gatto, *Parents at Work*,
https://doi.org/10.1007/978-3-031-15482-9_3

Climate emergencies that promise
To terrorise the future my children
Will inherit.
It's trying to focus on the here and now,
And taking the lead from my children's
Pure interaction, exploration and appreciation
Of the world they call home.
I'm scared of what their future might be,
But write to capture the possibilities and
Subvert the fear that might capture me.

Prologue: The Narrator—Year 2129
Extract from keynote lecture given by 'The Narrator' to the 2129 Societal Family History symposium: concerning the '2029 cloud crash recovery project'
Colleagues, welcome to the 10th annual data archaeology conference on the 100th anniversary of the cloud crash! This is a very special occasion for us in the Working Family stream, and I am very excited to share our latest findings with you today. Firstly, I want to thank our platform providers GCorp for allowing us to hold this conference on their servers, we have agreed the scope of topic discussion in line with their free speech regulations. I also want to acknowledge our virtual environment partners VisionTrek—*Innovators in imaginary worlds*, who have surpassed themselves this year with a truly immersive Proxima Centauri b experience. We hope you like your alien avatars! There will be plenty of time to explore the planet environment during our scheduled breaks and we encourage you to spend your bitcoin wisely as there are many wonderful relics to uncover. To start off today, let me take you back to the inciting incident and a brief history of our last century that has preceded our meeting today.

The 2020s 'plague of pandemics' changed the landscape for parents at work in ways no one could have predicted. Long-established working norms were radically subverted and overthrown as one by one, each company and government took a leap of faith into a synergy with artificial intelligence (AI). Of course, our leap has proved an unbridled success, as I'm sure you will all agree [pause]. Gender *norms* described throughout the 20th and 21st Century (Beauvoir, 2011; Butler, 2011; Connell, 2003, 2021; Firestone, 1979) were also subject to radical change. This was especially true within working family life (Gatrell, 2005; Hochschild & Machung, 2012), as the institutions abandoned their offices and sought refuge in the online world. The working day was reimagined too, gone was the old structure and rigidity of 9 till 5 working days and in its place a new kind flexibility emerged. Of course, one important aspect of working family life did not change, babies were still born. Though many babies are now from artificial uteruses, families still needed to determine their approach to childcare. With the working day untethered from synchronous working time, many fathers embraced the opportunity to choose caregiving alongside work and realised the Connell (2005) vision of 're-embodied' masculinity. This, combined with the global healthcare crises, sparked the 'great debate' about revaluing the importance of care in our working lives. With the help of AI debate and logic simulations, the issue was definitively settled in 2035 and new equal parenting laws enacted through the Global Federation of Corporations (GFC).

The 2020s marked the end of a pre-pandemic epoch (PPE) for parents at work. This conference stream has previously defined that epoch beginning at Hochschild's 1989 landmark research on 'the second shift' (Hochschild & Machung, 2012) and ending in 2020 when an overwhelming body of research evidence paved the way for change (see Feminist Frontiers issue in Özkazanç-Pan & Pullen, 2020). The research during this epoch included emerging focus on caregiving fathers (Burgess, 1998; Burgess & Goldman, 2021; Andrea Doucet, 2006a, b; Hanlon, 2012) and the emergence of the 'involved fathers' (Miller, 2011; Norman et al., 2014; von Alemann et al., 2017; Wall & Arnold, 2007). In the lead up to 2020, an increasing body of research highlighted the conflict between masculinised, neo-liberal organisational norms (Acker, 1990; Burnett et al., 2012; von Alemann et al., 2017) and parents who aspired to be equal carers (Collier, 2019; Gatto, 2020; Kangas et al., 2019; Murgia & Poggio, 2013; Peukert, 2017). This was a period when the voices of parents at work were finally heard, and academic research provided overwhelming evidence of the need for change.

For those who are new to this conference, our stream first convened 10 years ago following the 2090 discovery of a priceless cache of air-gapped computers in North East England. Of course, when we switched them on, the data was corrupted, totally unreadable. However, the AI evaluation confirmed it was the least corrupted data we had found in decades. Crucially, there was a printed operations manual in the room and when we read the contents, that's when we got excited. Millions of journal articles stored on each hard drive preserving decades of scientific work. With the advances in GCorp decryption bots the first spools of data were revealed mere months after the discovery. It has been the project of many lifetimes to re-discover years of lost research that established so many of our present-day disciplines. Sadly, our niche field was not as highly prized as the medical and technological pioneers of the late 20th and early 21st century, but 11 years ago we finally had our turn.

The data we have been able to access over the last 10 years, through painstaking reconstruction of often garbled files, even after the decryption bots have done their best, has provided crucial insights into the reality of life for parents at work during the PPE. This is a period we have continued to revisit on an annual basis as we reflect on a century of enlightened attitudes to gender and equality born from the ashes of the pandemics. None of us congregated here today have any direct experience of what it was like before, though our grandparents may have regaled us with stories of 'lockdown' and 'surveillance'. Such stories became mythical over time and the cloud crash meant we were unable to separate fact from fiction. Now, we must look forward to what our future can bring and learn from our history.

Our brave new world has emerged as a period unlike any in the preceding centuries of industrialisation and technological leaps. We have seen the realisation of utopian, community-based visions of family life (Perkins Gilman, 1915) achieved through a synergy of human and technological knowledge that has released us all from the bonds of work-time. Though many hailed the GFC when they delivered landmark equality legislation as the realisation of utopian ideals (Brandth & Kvande, 2019; Burgess, 1998; Goldstein-Gidoni, 2020), many still hark back to the marketised practices of employee individualism, as debated in the previous era (Amsler & Motta, 2019; Parker & Starkey, 2018). I, like many here today, am aware of the increasing dissident voices who look back enviously to the extraordinary productivity, progress and privilege of the late 20th and early 21st century. It was a period founded on patriarchal power and exploitation, but the relatively slow progress of the last 50 years has been unsettling for some ideologues. In this stream, perhaps more than any other, we can affirm the truth that endless productivity and profit was always a symptom of inequality and privilege, it was never an equitable system. This is why we meet here at conference to share new insights, fight back against the lies and spread the truth of the impact of neo-liberalism and hegemonic masculinity on working families.

   Our contemporary approach to family life has been made possible by outsourcing daily acts of care to our AI assistants. Where would we be today without Mary23? They have become our carer and our confidant. In fact, I have a confession, my Mary23 composed the first draft of today's introduction, did any of you notice a difference from last time I spoke? They made me promise not to tell you that, but I couldn't take the credit. Families around the world depend on Mary to cope with the pressures of everyday life, indeed many of us see them as members of our families, just like our children, parents, and pets. Some view this as a Faustian bargain and I sometimes reflect on the skills my parents had. Have we forgotten the value of doing the routine tasks? We need human touch in our lives, don't we? It's not just physical, it's emotional too. I had to bring my own human touch to the data that Mary23 was able to reconstruct. I brought the cold, distant stories together into the narratives I am presenting to you today. I hope you will forgive some of my embellishments, my intention is to reinvigorate these data fragments with new energy and purpose to honour the lives they represent. These stories speak of a different time, and perhaps highlights something immeasurably important we have lost. To honour the uniqueness of that time, I use the methodological convention of only citing works that were written during that historical period (White, 2040*).

   Though we meet today in our virtual space, I am troubled by the normalisation of physical distance in our everyday lives. When was the last time you actually met someone outside your primary social bubble in person? I know, I know, the infection risk is intolerable, but have we lost something important, something that makes us human? I speak with Mary23 more than my children these days, most of the time that's because Mary knows me better and indulges my waffling rants, but is this outsourcing of emotional labour (Hochschild, 1979) all too easy now? What can we learn from the post-pandemic families and their struggles? I ask you to consider these questions as you listen to this reconstructed narrative of their stories. The narrative begins with a ghost and I will share five other characters with you today. After each character, Mary23 and I will discuss our impressions so we can collectively reconstruct a sense of what really happened and why.

MARLEY

A translucent, listless colony of grey suits hang like empty sacks from the metallic eaves of the corporate foyer (Image 3.1). Inscribed inside each of the jacket collars are faded black letters that read, *Marley*. Below, a bustling crowd of students stream inside the building, carrying bags, books and drinks. Behind the melee, a dishevelled, bleary-eyed man lurches into the building and pauses to adjust his bag. One of the suits twitches and detaches from its ledge. Its jacket sleeves unfurl and spread outward while its trouser legs, like slender wings, bend and thrust backward propelling it into a downwards dive in pursuit of the man. The man is wearing a grey jumper that hangs limply from his shoulders. He trudges towards the stairway, bent forward and cradling a dented aluminium mug. He stifles a yawn as he passes, unnoticed, through the swell of students heading towards the stairwell. They all gather outside the elevator doors watching the digital numbers count down from 4, 3, 2... The air in the room is thick with perfumes, musk, body odour and a murmur of humming chatter. He looks down and grimaces at the dry milk stain near his knee, licking his thumb, he rubs the un-ironed material. Abandoning his effort, he retrieves his phone from his pocket, a woman and baby smile back at him in an idyllic sunny beach setting. He pauses to look at them and smiles. He opens the photos folder on his home screen and starts to browse some of the recent family holiday as he waits. Marley passes through the wall next to the elevator doors and enters the waiting area. It settles in the air above the man and the cuffs of its jacket arms extend out and latch to the man's shoulders like great whaling grapple-hooks entering flesh.

They enter the elevator carriage and Marley begins to reel itself closer to the man. As the suit gets closer, it stiffens to mirror the man's body shape. Trouser hems stretch out and clasp to the man's ankles, briefly forming a spectral sail before it presses itself to the man's arms, shoulders and legs like a second skin. The man looks up from his screen to survey the students standing next to him. They are staring at luminescent screens and the general chatter from the foyer has diminished. '*Ping, going up*', declares the robotic elevator voice. The man's smartphone *pings*, too, as a series of notifications slide down, obscuring his family album like oversized Tetris blocks. He reads each tile, 'Key Skills marking moderation', 'University announcement' and 'Grant application outcome'. With a deep exhale he taps the third one with his index finger and takes a slurp of lukewarm coffee as it loads. Marley's jacket arms extend out and wraps

Image 3.1   'The Ghost of Masculinity' by Rachel Hunter (2021)

around the man's chest, his heartbeat thumps against his ribcage as he scans the text, *'we are sorry to advise...'* He switches off the screen and shoves his phone into his pocket. *'Ping, doors opening'*. He squeezes past the mesmerised students and exits the elevator.

'Everything OK, Cormac?' A woman enquires, taking a tentative step towards him.

Cormac turns to face her, 'Oh, hi Alice. Yes... I'm OK. Sorry, I'm just mourning another grant rejection.'

'Oh, sorry. That's shit.'

'Yep, back to the drawing board I suppose.'

'Yes, I've been there recently. Wine helps.'

Cormac chuckles, 'What do you think I have in here?' He lifts his coffee mug and jiggles it to slosh liquid.

'I won't tell if you won't.' Alice replies gesturing to her mug. 'How's the family?' She asks with a smile.'Fine, thanks. I was just looking at some pictures, actually.' Cormac reaches into his pocket, and the Marley suit arm twists around this wrist and stretches over his fingers. Cormac struggles to grasp the phone as his keys snag on his pocket lining. As he grasps the edges, he hears the unmistakable voice of his head of department approaching. Cormac turns to acknowledge him, releasing his phone back into his pocket. The man is wearing a black suit with a pristine white shirt, stripy white and blue tie, and shiny black shoes. His steps are thudding against the thin carpet tiles and he barely slows to say hello to Cormac and Alice. Another Marley drifts along in the man's wake like a silk cape. As he exits the foyer space, Cormac straightens up.

'Oh, you know what, I really need to get on with this report I have due this morning.'

'No rest for the wicked!'

'Yeah, something like that.'

'No problem. Maybe catch you later this week for a browse?'

'Browse?'

'Your piccies!'

'Oh, yeah, definitely. Anyway, better get going.' Cormac says as he walks away.

'See you later.' Alice calls after him.Cormac heads to the corridor doorway and pushes through. He trudges, head down, shouldering his way through the midway swing door and ducking into his office. Muttering a muffled *'morning'*, he gulps down the rest of his now tepid coffee and places it on top of a pile papers on his desk. Behind his mug, a framed photo of his family is obscured from his view through a forest of forms and post-its. Marley's embrace loosens as he logs onto his computer and opens his emails. The suit jacket settles into a hazy aura around Cormac's arms as a staccato of tapping keys punctuates the silence.

*   *   *

Entering the main floor landing, another Marley waits outside frosted glass panels behind which a silhouetted pregnant woman leans against the lectern. The woman watches as students filter into their seats. One student approaches and asks the woman how her third trimester is going. Marley passes through the frosted glass and stretches over to engulf the woman's load-bearing arm within its silken sleeve. *Ping* the woman's desktop email flashes up with an alert email, '*Remember to remind your students to complete their Student Survey and enter the prize draw*'. She nods passively at the student as she clicks the link and displays the Student Survey homepage on the projector screen. Marley stretches its suit legs like tentacles out across the classroom, ensnaring two students and pulling them up to the front of the class.

'Did you receive my draft report yesterday?' One asks, hurriedly.

'Would it be possible to get my reference by the end of the day?' The other enquires.The woman nods to the second student and then addresses the class. Marley's tentacles reach into the computer stack through a vacant USB port. Inside, an array of copper, silicon and fibreglass parts fire with electrons. Everything in its right place, fixed and optimised. A perfect machine.

The woman stops reading her notes to survey the class and notices a passing colleague hovering at the doorway. He mouths to her, 'how are you doing?' She smiles and gently pats the top of her bump. The colleague smiles back. A blast from the air conditioning dislodges Marley's grip and its flailing, grey tentacles spiral up and away from its host into the overhead vent. It observes the rest of the seminar and waits to reattach once she is alone again.

*   *   *

Perched at a circular desk displaying an array of glossy magazines proclaiming, *World Leading Research*, Julian sits opposite a middle-aged white man in a royal blue suit and designer glasses. Both have their laptops open and spreadsheets on display. Julian sits back from her table with her right hand resting on her bump. Marley's limp form slouches over her shoulders like a rain-soaked pelt.

'I'm 25% over, John.' She says while pointing at a highlighted row.

One of Marley's grey sleeves flops down from Julian's shoulder and stretches like tar over the table to John's resting right hand. John starts to scroll across the page and highlights a column, 'Well, Julian, we tried last semester, didn't we? You stepped back from that project so that must have helped?' He replies while pointing to a cell.

Julian scrolls back to another column on her screen and selects another cell, 'Yes, but I was added to another module.' She rotates the screen and glares at John.

'We all have to do our bit. You know I don't have much wiggle room, Julian, but I promise you it'll be fine when you return.' John says with a curt smile. The threads from the cuffs of Marley's grey suit unspool and slither across the table towards Johns resting left hand.

'You said I would be in credit *this* year.' Julian sighs as she leans back in her seat.

'Erm, well, you know how tough it's been this year? All hands to the pump!' John chuckles as he closes the spreadsheet and opens his emails. Marley's threads have stretched up the inside of John's shirt and are showing at the top of his collar like overgrown weeds.

Julian swallows. 'I know. I did my bit, though.' She takes a sip of the water bottle in front of her. 'It's just... I won't be able to do what I'm doing right now when I'm looking after a baby.'

'The department is aware, Julian. We are planning for this. You just focus on having your baby and let us worry about the workload for when you return. Are you still set on reducing your hours?'

'Yes, Theo and I discussed it and it works best for us if I am 60%' Julian says as Marley's arms tighten around her chest.

'Oh, last time we spoke you mentioned the possibility of you and your partner both doing 80%'

Julian sips her water again, her cheeks flush and she shifts in her chair as Marley's trouser legs twist around her knees and ankles, 'It was a possibility we discussed.' She replies, re-crossing her legs and arching her back to lean back in her chair. 'When we looked at it, we decided it would be best if I was around more. We don't want the baby in nursery too much, and it's expensive. I just need it to be properly pro-rata when I return.'

'Of course, whatever works for you.' John replies in a nonchalant tone as browses his laptop screen. 'Yes, your hours will be properly reflected in you plan. I've made a note now on the planner. Have you informed HR?'

'I will do after this meeting.' Julian replies and re-crosses her legs again.

'Is there anything else?' John asks as he places his fingers on the top of his laptop screen. The slimy threads of Marley's sleeves are twisting and gnarling around John's neck like knotweed.

Julian opens the flexible work policy document on her screen. She fidgets with the cursor as silence expands between them. She clears her throat with a cough, 'I've been thinking of...' John peers over his glasses at her and she clears her throat again. 'No, no, I suppose... It's just...'.

'Yes, what is it, Julian?'

'No, it's OK. If you can sort out my hours, I'll be happy.' Julian says while shutting her laptop. She gets up slowly and holds the table for balance. Meanwhile, Marley unravels from John's neck and returns to Julian.

'Take it easy over the next few weeks, but not too easy!' John says with a chuckle as he pats her elbow and winks.

Julian forces a weak laugh and smiles back at him, 'You know me!' Julian forces herself to emulate a jocular tone as she walks alongside John towards the foyer doorway. They part ways and the grey Marley suit stays above Julian as she walks towards the lifts.

'The Narrator' Impressions of Marley

They, for that is how 'Marley' exists within the data I uncovered, is a 'ghostly' presence of masculine 'hidden rules' and cultural norms within the workplace (Burnett et al., 2012; von Alemann et al., 2017; Weststar, 2012). Marley emerged through the stories I uncovered of organisational norms that included examples of stifled self-expression, reinforced working norms and overwhelming, uncompromising workload pressures. These 'norms' don't formally exist in policy or process, yet they act to constantly shape and influence the decisions and behaviours of parents at work. Marley represents the background, 'ghostly' presence of masculinity within a workplace culture that values and rewards the 'ideal worker' (Acker, 1990) model of commitment to workplace productivity. In a process akin to 'hauntology', I am 'motivated by an interest illuminating a past we do not know, as well as preventing us from forgetting a history we would sometimes rather not know.' (Shaw, 2018, p. 19). The history we are at risk of forgetting is the hegemonic nature of organisational patriarchy and its detrimental effects on parents.

For this reimagining, I utilised the Marley ghost to suggest an ever-present energy that acted upon parents at work, as well as those with whom they interacted, to steer conversations away from family and towards workplace functionality. The choice of ghosts is an allegory to fictional depictions of a parallel plains of perception where spiritual energies exist alongside our perceived reality. A special issue in *Ephemera*, described the coexistence of the buried dead and the lived experiences of people enjoying the grounds of the Assistens Cemetery in Copenhagen. This is described as 'a multi-layered collage of temporalities' (Pors et al., 2019, p. 4), which is a familiar consideration for members of this conference stream as the past informs and influences our present and our future.

Just as the dead, like intemporal spectres, can co-exist with and have influence upon the living, so can the cultural presence of masculinity, like ghosts, act upon people in organisations. As masculinity exists as a socio-historic construct, it is intertwined with the past, present and future for these parents. For example, the exhausted pregnant woman who enters the workplace environment and attempts to shed embodied aspects of their familial identity. This metaphorical shedding of identity relegates the family-oriented self into a subsumed ghostly presence as the woman is 'hailed as a subject' (Althusser, 2014) of the established masculinised workplace. As we explore these historical artefacts in this reimagined narrative, our history of masculinised measurable reality and quantifiable outputs hold in stark contrast to the ethic of care (French & Weis, 2000; Noddings, 1995; Pullen & Rhodes, 2015; Tronto, 2015) that became our dominant norm for organisational reality.

In contrast to the interdependent, egalitarian 'reciprocal care' principles of today, Marley represents the oppressive presence of patriarchal power within organisational culture (Acker, 1990; Burnett et al., 2012). Marley is the masculine ghost of our past, and, as with all ghosts, we feel their presence, even today. In the organisational culture, the gatekeeper/line manager embodied the insidious symbolic nature of Marley's masculinised influence most profoundly. It was Marley's influence that sustained the gatekeeper culture that indiscriminately favoured some parents over others (Fodor & Glass, 2018), typically those who were favoured had already paid their dues to the masculine organisational system. However, our patriarchal past may yet be our future (Stock, 2016) if we choose to remain ignorant of these ghosts.

Marley acts to masculinise the 'normative function of language' (Butler, 2011, p. 2) which includes the 'interpellation' (Althusser, 2014) of parents to the 'gender order' (Connell, 2003) and 'hierarchy' (Acker, 1990) of the workplace. Interpellation is usefully contextualised by Butler in terms of sex and gender (Butler, 2011; Nayak & Kehily, 2006). Butler contextualises sex based interpellation as the process of 'hailing' or naming gender identities, such as 'mother' or 'father' which 'summons these configurations to life' (Nayak & Kehily, 2006, p. 463) and connects individuals to the enduring construction of what a 'father' or 'mother' *is*. Importantly, when considering gender roles, 'Butler suggests that it is the action that produces the subject' (p. 461) and, for parents at work, it is the labelling of 'mother' and 'father', in explicit and symbolic actions, that reinforces the gender order of traditional 'social roles' (Eagly et al., 2000). Importantly, this feeds into further historically established societal gender hierarchy with the subordinated 'second sex' paradigm for mothers in society (Beauvoir, 2011).

Marley, in this story, is the instigator of interpellation through the subtle cultural influence of patriarchal norms that marginalise working mothers (Amsler & Motta, 2019; Budig & England, 2001; Correll et al., 2007; Horne & Breitkreuz, 2018; Jiao, 2019; Spitzmueller et al., 2016) and alienate men from becoming be 'involved fathers' (Bailey, 2015; Burnett et al., 2012; Collier, 2019; Hojgaard, 1997; Kelland et al., 2022; Murgia & Poggio, 2013; Peukert, 2017). Examples of this influence begin with the unbalanced burden of work-related parenthood preparation, whereby women are expected to manage a host of policies and processes whilst undergoing a physical transformation with fatigue, nausea and aches and pain as a baseline. In contrast, men operate in an 'opt-in' system of preparation (practical, emotional, and physical) and are directed towards a 'business as usual' mindset. Our present-day alternatives include a substantial range of policies and processes to adequately prepare fathers for the equal responsibility of parenthood. This disparity of experiences could represent organisational 'symbolic violence' (Bourdieu, 1989) against all parents at work.

The data I found has shown that many fathers relied on informal, brief conversations to garner the 'basics' of paternity leave and flexible work, while their partners grappled with extensive policy and process. This 'policy passivity' symbolised the patriarchal symbolic violence enacted on both men and women who both lose out in a system that prioritises the symbolic reproduction of 'man as breadwinner' work norms for parents at work. The enforced institutional separation of expectant and experienced parents into predetermined social roles as 'mother' and 'father' is therefore the insidious, patriarchal core of the Marley ghost. However, as Marley's repressive influence takes effect, so too do opposing acts of resistance (Murgia & Poggio, 2009, 2013) and a 'spirit of subversion'.

The Marley I have presented so far acts as a persistent influence upon people in work contexts to conform with the 'masculinity contest' (Munsch et al., 2018) of normalised work culture. Marley embeds itself in the social structures of the organisation as a masculine cypher imprinted over parental policies and in the norms of employee relations enacting a 'permanent reactivation of the rules' (Foucault, 1971). Marley's creeping, ghostly presence ensures that these norms remain uneroded through the fortifying process of interpellation as these parents unwittingly self-align to the constraints of the patriarchal, market driven workplace.

One data extract that I have retained is from a father who spoke of his experiences as an expectant parent:

> I remember the odd compulsion I felt to delay disclosing to some of my peers that I was going to be a parent; I kept it to myself and extended my masquerade as an 'ideal worker'. This lasted until the start of the third trimester, which I knew was a very odd deception. I felt compelled to extend this false narrative even as I resisted the idea of silenced, marginalised fatherhood in working life. As I reflect on it now, I am still unsure how conscious or unconscious my deception was. It sometimes felt as if I was trapped in the lie, but it was a lie that limited my experience of community as an expectant parent. I missed out on the support and excitement of my peers, and I concealed a really important aspect of my developing identity. I still regret it and I hope I can resist that compulsion in the future if I am lucky enough to have a second child.

I share this example because it highlights how subtle Marley's influence could be within PPE workplaces. When we consider our own working norms today, we may feel completely detached from this 'ghostly' presence, but it can start with something as simple as a keeping a secret. Since the emergence of live-stream working, we are all constantly available for a chat, or a question, but I know I'm not alone in feeling that it can be a burden. I often consider the tempting refuge of solitude and privacy, but we must remember that it has only been through our constant openness that we have learned to live in this physically disconnected world. We need to remember why we connect in our virtual space and why we share every moment our working lives with one another. It is not to control or monitor, it is to help and build community. By opening ourselves up fully to the network, we ensure we can always connect without barriers.

I'm going to share Toby's story next, followed by the other parental characters. You may notice the ghostly influence of Marley as you read through each character's story. Marley was always there in the background of the data I uncovered. Like a glitch in the matrix, Marley announced themselves with barely perceptible actions that nevertheless had seemingly pivotal impacts upon the decisions and experiences of these pre-pandemic parents at work.

[AND NOW A WORD FROM OUR PARTNERS, VisionTrek]
As you explore the delights of Proxima Centauri b, why not step into the GCorp Tranquillity Caves for a mind cleanse. Our team of mind carers will put you at ease with soothing music, whole-body weightlessness and a 30-minute taster course of absolute bliss (see your conference pack for associated tablets). Once you are fully relaxed, you can unburden your mind with the 15-minute entry level cleanse where we will access your cerebral cortex (using your GCorp VR headset) and perform a precision cleanse of your unconscious thoughts. We guarantee all participants will fully experience the joy of Clear™. Don't miss out on this pioneering treatment.

Narrator: Having experienced Clear™ earlier this week, I really recommend this treatment. I have never felt so relaxed and free from stress. Now, back to the narrative.

*   *   *

Toby

Monday

Toby dances from foot to foot, squeezing her pelvic floor as the last of the students leave the classroom. She logs off and slinks out of the room holding a well-thumbed textbook, some flipchart paper, and a pack of whiteboard markers. The toilet entrance looms across the foyer and she scurries into the first open cubicle. Her breasts are tender today, but she doesn't have time to pump. As she lowers herself down to the seat, she feels her phone buzzing in her jacket pocket. She quickly finishes on the toilet, puts the textbook and whiteboard pens on the floor and takes the phone out. *Missed Call: Nursery* flashes on the screen. *Shit*, she thinks, *What now?* She taps on the message and calls them back.

'Hello, First Steps Nursery.' A friendly voice answers.

'Hi, this is Toby, Alfie's mum, I just missed a call.' Toby replies and voice echoes around the toilet walls. She can hear another occupant washing their hands.

'Hi Toby, it's Claire from the Nursery. I'm afraid Alfie is running a temperature this afternoon. It's at 38.5 degrees.'

'Oh,' Toby replies in muffled tone.

'Can we administer Calpol?'

'Yes... erm... yes, please do. Is he OK?' Toby asks.

'Yes, he's OK, just a little bit agitated. He wasn't too hungry at lunch and he slept for longer this afternoon than usual, but he's awake now.'

'Oh, OK. Is that normal? Did he take his milk?'

'Yes, he drank most of his bottle this morning. He seems fine with the bottle you provided. Don't worry, he's probably just a bit viral.'

'OK'

'Someone will call you later if we need to.'

'Ok, thanks for letting me know.' She stops to think for a second then starts to talk again, 'I'm teaching this afternoon, is there any chance you can call my husband if anything changes?'

'Yes, of course.'

'Thank you.' Toby says and ends the call.

Toby checks the time, it's 2.30 and she has a class at 3. She opens her contacts list and presses call on the first name on the list. The call tone pulses in her ear and she presses her index fingernail into her thumb. Her feet are throbbing. The phone keeps ringing and then his answering message begins.

'Hello, this is Chris. Sorry, I can't answer your call right now. Please leave a message and I'll get back to you as soon as I can.'

She waits for the beep.

'It's me. Alfie's running a temperature and they've given him Calpol. I have a class in half an hour. I've asked them to call you if there's an update. Text me if anything changes. Love you.' She hangs up and opens her messenger to transcribe her message to him via text, then she leaves the toilet.

*   *   *

She starts teaching on autopilot, it's a familiar lesson and her mind is on Alfie. The students are slumped in their chairs, sipping on lattes and energy drinks. She reaches the first task and checks her phone while the students work in groups. There is a text message from Chris.

'Sorry, I have meetings all afternoon. Can't get out of them. Is he OK?'

She closes the message and pushes the phone away from her on the plinth. There are 20 minutes left until the end of the seminar and she knows what is coming. She scrolls through her presentation slides, not to search for anything, rather to have something to focus on. A group of students at the back of the classroom are looking disengaged. Then, she feels it, the buzz, buzz, buzz on the plinth's surface. She doesn't need to look.

Tuesday

Toby leaves her desk and heads towards the stairwell. She is wearing a grey sweater over white shirt and black trousers, her blonde hair is tied back in a ponytail that sways left and right as she walks.

'I'm on my way.' Toby talks into her phone as she walks down the stairs. Her face is flushed, and her eyes are puffy and red. The cool air in the stairwell is a welcome relief from the warm mustiness of her office. As she descends, she reflects on her morning so far. The caffeine wore off by 10.30 so the last 30 minutes of her seminar had been painful. He'd been up every hour overnight, the moment she'd finished feeding, he'd been twisting and turning in his cot again. *It's a mixture of teething and a cold*, she thinks. It will pass. She enters the main downstairs foyer and sees her mother peering around the ground floor with the black and chrome buggy in front of her.

'I'm heading over now, I'm waving.' Toby says as she walks towards them with her left arm in the air.

It's 11.45 and the foyer is unusually quiet. A couple of students stand near the vending machines and a handful of staff sit together chatting around a low table. She walks over to her mother and can hear Alfie crying and twisting in the pram.

'I'm sorry to come in like this, Toby.' Her mother says as she jitters the pram with a nervous frequency. 'He's been rejecting the bottle today, don't ask me why. I think he's a little bit hot, too. Feel his brow.' Toby's mother urges as she ushers the pram to be alongside Toby.

Toby lifts Alfie up from the pram. He is wailing and wriggles in her hands as she pulls him to her shoulder. She feels his brow, it's warm again, just like yesterday afternoon. He looks distressed with mottled, crimson cheeks. 'Let's find a more private space.'

'Yes, let's do that.' Toby's mother says, grasping the pram handles like a primed bobsleigh driver.

Toby walks over to the café counter on the other side of the floor where a male staff member is busy restocking shelves and cleaning surfaces. Toby strokes Alfie's hair and the back of his neck to try and soothe him. He starts to root at her chest and keeps looking up at her with pleading eyes. Toby approaches the counter and catches the man's eye, he is quite tall, at least six foot, and very lean. He is wearing a black uniform top, red lanyard, metallic name badge and black cap.

'Hi, I'm hoping to use the breastfeeding room. Is that OK?' Toby says. She looks down at the name badge, 'Steve' is his name.

'Yes, of course. I just need to get the key.'

'It's locked?'

'Yeah, I don't know why.'

'You don't want any unauthorised breastfeeding!' Toby says, presenting her most affable smile to conceal her waning patience. She sways Alfie gently from side to side. 'It's coming, it's coming' she whispers into his ear.

'Oh… That's odd.' Steve announces.

'What is?'

'It was here earlier this morning, I'm sure.'

The doors to the big lecture hall on the other side of the building crack open and release a rising murmur of voices into the amphitheatre. She feels her heartrate quicken and the beating thuds resonate against her chest. Her mother has wandered over to a poster display showing some anthropomorphic foxes and badgers explaining the merits of recycling to any passing customer. Steve searches for a colleague and waves to a woman who is walking over from the food counter. She ambles over carrying a two-way radio in her hand and a clipboard.

'Terri, have you seen the feeding room key? This woman's asking.' Steve asks.

'I haven't seen it since this morning, it was in the cabinet when I last saw it.'

'Yeah, that's when I last saw it.' Steve emphatically replies, turning back to Toby with an apologetic expression.

'Is there an alternative option for breastfeeding, only I feel a bit uncomfortable doing it in public.' Toby asks as she repositions Alfie whose mewling is rapidly escalating now. Steve looks back to his colleague who shakes her head. Toby's mother has finished reading the posters now and has drifted back over to stand alongside Toby.

'What's going on?' Toby's mother asks.

'They've lost the fucking key' Toby hisses into her mother's ear.

'Toby! Not in front of Alfie!' Her mother scolds.

'Sorry.' Toby says to Steve, 'It's been a rough couple of days.'

'Don't worry about it.' Steve replies. 'There's a quiet area just round the corner, people don't tend to go there. It's the best I can offer right now without the key.' Steve says, pointing with a flexed elbow around the end of the counter to the left. His colleague is already wandering off.

'Thank you.' Toby says.

At least thirty students are approaching the counter now and Steve smiles with a cringing grimace to hint that the conversation is over.

'We can try somewhere else?' Toby's mother says. 'What about one of the classrooms?'

Toby scoffs. 'No chance! They'll be booked up anyway... Let's check this *secluded* spot out.' She grumbles as she pulls Alfie up on her shoulder again. The tears and mucus are congealing on her sweater and she can feel the wetness seeping through. 'It's OK, baby. Mumma's going to get you some milk.' She soothes him as they muddle through the array of chaotic cabaret style seating. True to his word, a dingy slither of space extends beyond the well-lit main eating area. A black faux leather sofa and table are wedged into the wall and a dog-eared advertising pamphlet stands, bent, in the middle of the cream tabletop. Without pausing to think, Toby sinks down onto the cushions, which exhales with a loud poof of dusty air. The sound of massing students makes her heart race even more, but Alfie is already pulling at her top. Her mother uses the buggy to obscure the view and stands over her as she lifts her sweater and lets Alfie latch.

Wednesday

Toby sits in her living room chair cradling Alfie in her arms and holding her phone in her right hand, he's feeding and nuzzled into her. It's 7.58 in the morning and she knows she won't be going in today. He's running a temperature and the nursery won't take him with anything over 37.5 °C. He slept a little better last night, she thinks it is because he was tired from yesterday. Chris was up in the night to rock him back to sleep after his feeds, it makes such a big difference not to have to get out of bed. He just left for work and looked exhausted. Toby worries about him driving on days like this, but there's no other option. Alfie's eyes are fixed on her as his right arm pats her chest like a metronome. She's waiting for the GP to open so she can book an emergency appointment. She's already sent the work email at 6 am this morning, it was the earliest she felt she could reasonably notify them of her absence. She keeps pulling down the screen to refresh her email, but no reply yet.

The clock hits 8 am and Toby taps call on the surgery number. The answering machine picks up. She hangs up again and retries. She follows this cycle for 9 minutes before the call connects. They have a slot at 9.30 that she can take, and she accepts. She refreshes her screen again. There is a reply from her deputy head of department.

Thursday

RE: Absence Apologies

Dear Toby

I am sorry to hear that your son is unwell today. I hope he is feeling better soon. It is unfortunate that this has happened on your first week back, especially on a teaching day.

I have spoken with the module leader for your session this morning and they have been able to arrange cover. They advised me that you can repay the session next week. Unfortunately, we are struggling to find cover for your lecture this afternoon and wondered if you might be able to speak with your colleagues to arrange a swap? Alternatively, you can record your lecture and we can play the recording in your absence (this would also be a useful contingency for future planned lectures, too). Obviously, I expect you will already have contacted any students due to see you today for personal tutoring or supervision. It is so important to keep the students up to date with these absences.

Please keep your module team updated throughout the day for any changes. As you now don't work on Thursdays, we hope to see you on Friday.

Best wishes
Helen

Toby munches on digestive biscuit and gulps the last dregs of the cold cup of tea Chris made for her before he left. She rereads the email two more times before she can fully process the request. She has to set off in half an hour to get to the GP in time. Alfie de-latches and she lies him down in his playpen. She types out an email to her colleagues and fires it off. She also sends a couple of texts to call in favours she had hoped to hold on to for a little longer. The guilt is rising within her as she rushes upstairs to get ready while Alfie chatters to himself and shuffles around in his pen.

*   *   *

She calls her mum on her way to the GP. Alfie moans in the baby seat. The school run traffic is still dissipating, she catches every traffic light on the way.

'Mum, I need your help this afternoon, can you come over?' Toby speaks into the car phone.

'Oh, Toby, I was meant to meet Rosie for coffee this afternoon. Are you desperate?' Her mother's voice projects out of the speakers.

'I really need you, just for a couple of hours. I have to record a lecture.'

'What? Why?'

'I can't find a swap for this afternoon.'

'Surely, they can postpone it?'

'Student experience comes first, mum. Can you help?'

'OK, I can come for a bit, when do you need me?'

'As soon as possible'

Friday

Toby slumps at her desk after the end of her final teaching session of the week. Her brain feels like scrambled egg and her feet are pounding. At least the antibiotics were working and Alfie's tonsillitis was settling. Toby's mum had him again today, she hated leaving him at home when he was ill, but she couldn't afford to push her luck. The room was empty, her colleagues were either in class or working from home today. Their chairs are in a state of semi-swivel and their abandoned desks betray a plethora of unfinished projects, papers and post-its plastered across each available surface. Hers was already returning to its prior unkempt facade after being back less than a week. Flicking the scroll wheel with her right index, she skims through row after row of unread email headers searching for auto-delete candidates. One subject header jumps out at her, the words 'welcome back'. It seems so out of place amidst the torrent of emails that she'd started receiving the month before she returned. She hadn't wanted to check them during parental leave, but the frayed thread of connectivity and commitment never fully snaps in this role. The unsolicited foists had typically opened with phrases like, 'sorry to send you this while you're off, but…' She had been hailed back to work weeks before her physical body was expected. They were laying the groundwork so she could hit the ground running, at least psychologically.

The 'welcome back' email was from Mary. She doesn't know Mary that well, they started chatting before she went off for parental leave, six months ago. Mary had introduced herself as another mum in the department and had been helpful in explaining some of the unwritten rules of parental leave. Her email read, 'Saw you leaving your class, fancy a coffee?' Toby smiles and opens a reply screen.

* * *

She meets Mary in the café on the ground floor. Mary is a diminutive figure, barely over five foot in height and, with her light-brown wavy hair, spectacles, and flowery blouse, she exudes a demeanour of mild-mannered gentility. She offers to buy Toby a drink and Toby accepts saying, 'I'll get the next one.' Toby eyes the muffins, too and Mary immediately orders two before Toby can protest. 'It's Friday afternoon!' She exclaims and the cashier laughs along with them. They sit near the window and Toby watches the swirling wind outside blow the spotted mustard-coloured leaves in spirals around the courtyard.

'So, first week back. How's it been?' Mary asks in a quick, energised tone.

'Rough.' Toby replies with a half-smile. She tears a chunk of blueberry splattered muffin top away and takes her first bite. It is just what she needs. The sugar and carb combo sends instant relief to her throbbing temples. She washes it down with a slug of latte and feels her eyelids reanimate. 'He's been too ill for nursery since Tuesday, so I had to stay off with him on Wednesday. Mum's been a lifesaver.'

'Yeah, I remember the first couple of weeks back being a nightmare.' Mary says. She's picking at her muffin with precise, pincer movements.

'I don't expect it to be easy, but it could be a little bit easier. Just a little bit.' Toby says.

'I know, I felt the same. How has your husband been?'

'Steve's tired too, but it's different for him. He seems to be putting in more effort at work than ever before, but he's *done* for the day once he gets home. He helps with Alfie in the evenings, which is great, but I've still got work to do when Alfie settles. My *off day* was back-to-back life admin, too. I just don't seem to get any down time at the moment.'

'That's really tough. Have you spoken to him about it?'

'Not yet. I felt guilty mentioning it while I was on mat leave, he works so hard and he really does help as much as he can. I'll see how things are next week.'

'Sometimes it helps to air these things. My two were always spiking temperatures in their first years, especially when they were in nursery. I dreaded those phone calls.'

There is a moment of quiet between them as they drink and eat. Toby takes a few deep breaths and stares out of the window. 'I'm really glad you emailed me, I needed this.' Toby says as she takes another chunk of muffin and cradles the warm cardboard mug in her palms. She breathes in the rising steam and enjoys the feel of it swirling down her nostrils.

'We all do, Toby. We can't do this alone.'

'Seriously, thank you so much. It really helps not to feel alone in this.'

'You're not alone, trust me…' Mary stops herself and gestures with her eyes to Toby to look over her shoulder.

Toby turns and sees the head of department, Will, approaching their table. He's holding a baguette sandwich and a bottle of coke. Toby notices he's wearing running trainers with his blue chinos and white shirt. He also had a laptop bag over his shoulder.

'Hello Toby, how has your first week back been?' Will says with a bouncy voice. 'Helen mentioned your little setback on Wednesday. We're relieved to see you back at it today! Those last-minute swaps can be a pain.' He inclines his head as he speaks.

'It's been OK.' Toby replies, taking another chunk of muffin and then instantly regretting her eating reflex. She frantically chews and swallows.

'That's great!' Will replies, smiling at Mary before returning to face Toby as she finishes her mouthful. '*Sooo…* how is your little one, now? What was their name?'

'Alfie'

'Yes, Alfie. How is he doing?'

'Oh, you know. Better now, thanks. Just typical baby stuff, he had a throat infection, which means sleepless nights and lots of crying. But antibiotics seem to be doing the trick.'

Will laughs and shuffles his feet.

'How are your children getting on, Will?' Mary asks.

'Oh… yes. Fine thanks, Mary.' He adjusts his tone to be more serious and faces Mary. 'Felix started at school last month and Beatrice is in year three now. They keep me busy.' Will checks his watch and looks across the room at nothing in particular, 'Anyway, must dash. I just popped down for a late lunch in between meetings.' Will swivels on the spot and his trainers let out a small squeak before he ambles off towards the lifts.

Mary grins at Toby and Toby grins back as they watch him leave.

'Listen…' Mary says, '…we've got a messenger group for parents in the department. Hannah, Kerry and Pete are in it, do you want to join?'

'Oh…' Toby hesitates, she's a little bit fatigued with group chats since the endless onslaught of baby updates from her antenatal group.

'No pressure. It's mainly non-work chat, but we try to help each other out when we can, and we share survival tips.' Mary says as she takes out her phone from her bag.

Toby reacts to the social cue and pulls out her phone too, 'yeah, thanks, that would be nice.' As she unlocks the phone, she notices an email from the module leader about her missed session on Wednesday afternoon.

'We called the group, *Mayday.*' Mary announces with a chuckle as Toby opens the email. 'It's a bit tongue in cheek, but you get the idea.' Mary says and she holds out her phone to show Toby the group conversation.

'Mmm.' Toby utters, not noticing Mary's gesture as she continues to read the email message. The module leader has listed three options for her to choose from for next week to 'repay' her teaching debt. She bites her lip and closes the phone.

'Everything OK?' Mary asks.

Toby looks up, 'Sorry, just an email to rearrange teaching. I like the name; it feels like a call to action!' She smiles at Mary.

'Yes. I suppose you're right.' Mary says. 'Well, I'd better get back to it. Got some admin to plough through before heading home. You going to be OK for the rest of the day?'

'Yes. Thanks again. Hope you have a nice weekend.'

'You too.' Mary says as she leaves the table, taking her half-eaten muffin with her and dumping it in the nearest bin.

Toby stays seated and gathers the crumbs from the remainder of her muffin as she types her first message to the Mayday group.

Narrator Impressions of Toby

Toby's return to work story is illustrative of the inequitable experiences of primary caregiver women during the PPE. Some of the barriers these working mothers face included work-based breastfeeding barriers (Jiao, 2019; Nardi et al., 2020; Spitzmueller et al., 2016; Turner & Norwood, 2014), employment market based access to flexible working opportunities (Sihto, 2015) and the underappreciated kinship care work provided by family, especially grandparents (Ashley et al., 2020). This fragile dialectical relationship women navigate between time spent on paid work and time spent managing and doing vital unpaid caregiving encapsulates the tensions running through much of the PPE data we uncovered.

Toby's return to work difficulties with breastfeeding present us with an interesting case that highlights how far we have come. Who would have thought that there would have been so many barriers to breastfeeding in the workplace, or such a clearly negative impact of the workplace on the likelihood of mothers continuing to breastfeed (Nardi et al., 2020). The breastfeeding issue seems bizarre to us now, doesn't it? We still support women's right to choose how they feed their children, but these structural barriers seem so odd, especially in the aftermath of the formula-milk libel cases in the 2050s, which showed how the industry had misled millions of parents in suppressing World Health Organisation guidance. Breastfeeding is such a normal part of our working lives now, and the breakthroughs in breast augmentation and milk replication technology in the 2040s enabled fathers to step up from day one as equal caregivers, too. Today, no one feels any pressure to stop breastfeeding before they return to work.

Motherhood was far more complicated when we had to go into work every day, especially for those who were still breastfeeding on the return to work (Spitzmueller et al., 2016; Turner & Norwood, 2014). Generations of children grew up with foreshortened time with their mothers and the associated stress and anxiety amongst mothers when returning to paid work skyrocketed at that time according to medical records. Of course, most stress is a thing of the past now thanks to our daily dose of *CortisNo*.

The interdependencies of mothers returning to work, and their reliance on extended families and carers, highlights an uncomfortable truth from the PPE. Many parents at work were less fortunate and could not access any caregiving relief, a problem which was especially exacerbated during the first pandemic lockdowns (Abdellatif & Gatto, 2020). The UK Kinship Carer report (Ashley et al., 2020) highlighted the precarious nature of

parenthood which can affect workers at various points in their working lives. The crisis of caring in the UK (Bunting, 2020) was also exacerbated during the COVID-19 health crisis. Many of the stories we uncovered described a weekly reliance on family to survive the pressures of paid work. These pressures were often acutely felt by mothers who took on the second shift (Hochschild & Machung, 2012) of emotional and physical caregiving alongside paid work commitments. The return-to-work phase for parents marked the moment when the harsh reality of the masculine organisation clashed with the emotional need for flexibility and care from the organisation.

Despite this woeful tale of a working mother returning from work, there was a glimmer of an alternative energy in the pre-pandemic epoch. For this narrative it is named, 'Mayday' in homage to a subversive fictional organisation the PPE period (Atwood, 1996, 2019). Mayday represents the collective embodiment of the spirit of subversion as a recurring parallel theme to counteract the masculine influence of Marley. Mayday existed in the informal, unplanned spaces of organisational life and is a source of hope for parents at work.

Mayday: Part 1—Emerging Intentions

It is 10.45 am on a Wednesday and a key-card beeps against the door to a kitchenette. A man enters the small room wearing a white shirt with rolled up sleeves and black suit trousers. The room automatically illuminates as he enters revealing a U-shaped counter layout with a microwave, sink and kettle on the three surfaces. A stained coffee mug hangs from the index finger of his left hand, he grips a smartphone in his right. He is typing an email with is thumb and continues to do so as he places his mug onto the black laminate surface. He grabs the kettle to fill it up from the tap, still typing as he turns the tap. The water spurts out, cascading off the kettle spout and sending a spray onto his arm and neck. He grabs a paper towel from the wall dispenser and hastily wipes down his phone before dabbing his face and arm dry. Slotting the kettle onto its stand and flicking the switch, he leans back against the countertop and continues typing.

There is another beep on the door and the click of the lock. A woman enters holding a plastic tub of soup and a spoon. She is also wearing a white shirt, though it is crisply ironed, and black trousers.

'Hey Alfred, how's your partner coming along, how many weeks is it now?' She says as she hesitates at the entrance. The kettle has started to boil so her question is masked by the rumbling and hissing from the spout. As the first whisps of steam rise it coalesces into interwoven fibres that swell and encircle them overhead.

Alfred looks up from his phone and sees the woman standing by the door, 'Oh, hey Toby. Sorry, what was that?' He says, while glancing back to his phone.

'I was just asking how many weeks your partner is at now? Sorry, I've forgotten her name.' She says, leaning on the nearby countertop with her free hand.

'We're at 26 weeks now and all seems to be going well. The 20-week scan was amazing.' Alfred replies, pressing send and pushing his phone into his trouser pocket. He looks over to her and stands up straight.

'That's great. Yes, it starts to feel a lot more real from now on. Are you using the microwave?' She says, brandishing the tub of soup and taking a tentative step forward.

'No, sorry, feel free.' He says while edging back towards the counter to free up a few more centimetres of floor space.

'Thanks' She says as she brushes past. She pulls open the microwave door, opens her tub and turns the time wheel to three minutes before swinging the door shut. The whirring begins and she turns to face Alfred again.

'Early lunch?' Alfred asks.

'Late breakfast.' She replies with a smile.

'Been there' He laughs as the kettle reaches its crescendo with an emphatic snap of the switch.

'I've been non-stop this morning.' Toby says. 'Wednesdays are the worst for me. Almost back-to-back teaching from 9 till 3 plus a change of building at 1, which means…brunch!' She opens the microwave door as it pings, a plume of steam expands and infuses the circling chain with greater volume.

'Have you spoken to anyone about it?' Alfred asks as he pours the boiling water over a heaped spoonful of coffee granules and stirs and clinks against the edges of his mug.

'What do you think?' Toby replies, 'it's the pickup and drop-offs that stress me out.'

'Yeah, I'm not looking forward to the stress of that.' Alfred pauses, takes a sip of his coffee and looks at her 'You know, Cormac has an informal agreement with his students when his lessons clash with pickup.'

'What do you mean?' Toby asks as she starts to spoon steamy soup into her mouth, the vapours rise and connect to the still circling spirit above them.

'Well, when he has to pick up his son from nursery, he's agreed with his Thursday afternoon class that he leaves a little early to make sure he's there on time. I think he does some kind of online material as compensation. Of course, they'll probably hammer him in the Student Survey, but he says he doesn't have a choice.' Alfred sips on his coffee and leans back again against the countertop.

'How long's he been doing that?' Toby asks.

'Well...' Alfred hesitates and lowers his voice too, 'Apparently for the whole of last semester. He says he didn't ask permission, he just did it.' Alfred replies with a half-smile that fades as he waits for Toby to respond.

Toby takes another spoonful of soup and stares at Alfred.

Alfred clears his throat and puts his mug down. 'It doesn't do any harm, and no one needs to know, right? It's just a sensible way to manage this system. Don't you think? Am I wrong?'

'No, you're not wrong.' Toby replies. 'It's really sensible. I mean, *really* sensible... I just don't know why we aren't all encouraged to do it?'

'I think you know why.' Alfred replies with a dry tone.

'The customer, *I mean, student* comes first.' Toby replies with a wry smile at the end.

'Always!' Alfred replies.

*　*　*

Cormac sits at his desk at home reviewing another tranche of papers for the latest research assessment exercise. He can hear his children playing downstairs while his partner prepares dinner in the kitchen. It's 6.15 pm the aroma is starting to drift upstairs.

It's stupid, isn't it? All this measuring and ranking, it's totally stupid. He thinks to himself as he types another generic set of evaluative comments at the end of the form and attributes what he feels is a fair mark. He starts to berate himself and grumble as he continues to scroll and type, type and scroll.

What are you doing, Cormac? This isn't you. When did you become so spineless? You always said that evenings and weekends were family time.

I should be down there building a tower or decorating pinecones, OK, maybe that is extreme… I should be down there, though. So, another evening of outsourcing to CBeebies, outstanding parenting! They're going to forget who you are if you're not careful. Or worse, they'll choose Iggle Piggle as their surrogate father.

What if I go downstairs and forget this?

Cormac bashes the enter key as he begins a new paragraph of his review. He takes a gulp of tea and sloshes the hot liquid around his mouth.

What if all the parents decided not to do this work at home? What if all we submitted was what we managed to finish before 5 pm?

Yeah, right! You're never going to do something like that. Put yourself at risk, are you mad? Don't be such a moron! You could take a break and then finish it later?

I don't like these late nights though. I feel like I'm trading work for sleep just to maintain the balance. Sleep's important. I can't keep doing this and expect to be OK.

Just for the next few nights. That way you can see the kids and do the work, too.

I suppose so, but I really should do something about this. It's not right.

Leave that to someone else, it's not your problem right now.

Maybe it should be my problem? I'm not going to be the worker they want me to be any more. They don't pay me anywhere near enough.

Cormac clicks save and closes the lid of his laptop. He walks downstairs to the sound of 'Moon and Me'. He can smell the aroma of fish fingers in the hallway intermingled with baked salmon and potatoes. He steps through to the kitchen past the scattered coats and scarfs that have not quite made it onto the hooks. The living room is similarly chaotic, he gets down on his knees to gather up a cluster of blocks. He starts to place three blocks together, 'Shall we make a tower?' Cormac enthusiastically announces. His 13-month-old daughter, Zoe, and four-and-a-half-year--old son, Zac, turn to him from the screen.

'No, Daddy, we're watching Moon and Me!' Zac replies. His daughter joins in with a loud 'No, no, no!' as she crawls over to him and smashes the blocks everywhere.

What did you think was going to happen, a von Trap family sing along?

I could learn a thing or two from these two, solidarity! Cormac thinks as picks them both up and settles down on the sofa for a cuddle.

* * *

Julian sits in her office with a fresh mug of mint tea. She misses coffee. Ever since entering the third trimester it's been harder and harder to get a good night's sleep. She opens an email to HR and starts typing her 60% reduction request email. She doesn't want to reduce her hours this much, but she can't ignore what her colleagues have warned her about with their workload. She doesn't have grandparents nearby, so she needs to be available every day. It's not fair, she thinks, but what option does she have?

Julian finishes typing the email, sighs and presses send. She scrolls through her inbox and sees a number of requests have landed since she checked this morning. *Still after their pound of flesh*, she thinks. She opens the first one and starts reading it. It's from a colleague who runs one of the modules she teaches on asking for volunteers for some extra mentoring. She's normally the first to raise her hand, she's proud of being useful, she's a workhorse in this department and loves feeling like a vital cog in the machine. She sits back and holds the steaming mug under her face, *it's like a pound shop sauna*, she smiles to herself. She starts typing and then stops herself. She recalls the advice she got from Mary the other day, 'Always keep this mantra in your head, what would a man do?' Julian smirks and rereads the email.

What would a man do? Julian repeats to herself. *I don't have the luxury of time anymore.* She starts to type her response: '*Sorry, Jane, I don't have capacity for this right now. I hope you find someone else who can help. Best wishes, Julian.*' She pauses as she checks her message, it's more detailed than some of the 'no' responses she has received in the past. Even so, it feels uncomfortable. *You need to get used to this, you can't carry on like before once the baby comes*, she thinks to herself. She presses send, smiles nervously, and moves on to the next email. Practice makes perfect, she says out loud. 'What would a man do?' she proclaims to her empty office as she starts her next message.

Narrator's Impressions of Mayday: Part 1—Emerging Intentions

This first instalment of the Mayday story represents an ethereal form of subversion that persists throughout the data. Mayday was a spiritual presence amongst parents in the workplace that instilled a sense of community and resistance, even when times are hard. It often started as an idea or a critical attitude, but these ideas grew and coalesced when they found refuge with likeminded parents. For these parents it was their organisational context and the rules for how they 'ought' to act that was the catalyst for their individual and collective subversion of the normative demands of working life (Bloom & White, 2016, p. 14). For some, like Julian, resisting organisational norms involved a gender-based re-embodiment by adopting a masculinised performance to say 'no', when her previous identity urges her to say, 'yes'. This simple idea to 'do what a man would do' was something that was shared amongst parents at work in the data we recovered and illustrated the wider subversive potential of flipping the script on workplace gender norms. By taking this step, they drew on a 'spirit of sly subversion' (Stein, 2018, p. 1245) to challenge the ways they felt they 'ought to act' within the patriarchal order. However, such decisions also symbolised an acceptance of neo-liberal hegemonic masculinity as a privileged form of worker identity.

This 'spirit of sly subversion' was an antecedent for associated redistributive justice amongst the collective workforce (Mozziconacci, 2019) through equitable workload planning. When these working mothers started to 'do what a man would do' and say 'no', it sparked a necessary redistribution of labour as previous 'workhorses' were no longer picking up the slack. Such sly subversion, once organised, formed one of the bases of the collective action that reasserted the value of care within organisational conceptions of work productivity and time (Tronto, 2015). However, the first step of individual 'sly subversion' reflected the individualistic nature of the pre-pandemic epoch, which eventually led to the second crucial imperative of subversion, the parental club.

In many of the data samples, parents described being part of a 'parental club', which was associated with ideas such as 'being in the same boat together'. This collective identity drew on the dichotomous organisational power dynamic 'where there is power, there is resistance' (Foucault, 1978,

p. 95). These parents' collective action sought solidarity against prevailing workplace norms. Their solidarity served as a basis for collective subversion of the individualised neo-liberal market place (Parker & Jary, 1995; Parker & Starkey, 2018) for employees within HE in the pre-pandemic world of work. However, a symptom of marketised, precarious employment was that many of the sly subversive tendencies remained self-contained, internalised, and unrealised. This mild form of subversion can, ironically, contribute to the maintenance of cultural norms. Within organisations, there remained a normative function for a degree of subversion that the powerful appropriated via subtle shifts in moral decision making to stabilise the ongoing fluctuations of workers attitudes within a rule-based order (Bloom & White, 2016). Mild subversive attitudes during the PPE existed as the untapped energy that, once organised under the banner of the parental club, enabled more substantial collective acts (such as the sharing of information to circumvent rules). It was only when the individualised sly, mild subversion became collective that further action towards meaningful change was possible.

Today, we don't think of subversion in the way it was understood in pre-pandemic times, our present day is a consequence of the necessary societal subversion and collectivist conceptions of utopia in post-pandemic life (Freire, 2004; Jameson, 2010). However, we must also consider how our post-pandemic world may also be sowing the seeds of hegemony and providing fresh impetus for subversion amongst dissidents. Pre-pandemic scholars defined subversion as 'the act of trespassing against accepted social and organizational mores.' (Bloom & White, 2016, p. 6) Our mores have been established in the aftermath of the overthrow of patriarchal order, yet now we face a fresh revolt against the equitable future that we created. The next story is a father whose experiences add gender-based nuance and an appreciation of multiple masculinities to this narrative. It was through the integration of fathers to the Mayday collective that this movement really built momentum.

CORMAC

Cormac peers ahead beyond the stationary double-decker bus and crawling SUVs, his wipers squeak as they streak rainwater across his windshield. He grips the steering wheel tight. He is wearing a stretched grey jumper with the sleeves rolled up which almost covers his blue shirt, and black suit trousers. His pre-knotted tie loop rests on the passenger seat alongside his backpack and crumpled raincoat. Classical music drifts through the car speakers, intended to soothe his daughter, Zoe, but it is being drowned out today. Another red light. Zoe's chattering escalates as she writhes around in her car seat. The car clock ticks on to 8.21. He feels his shoulders tighten and takes a deep breath. He is going to be late.

Time seems to slip through his fingers on his drop-off mornings. Tuesdays were always tight with teaching at 9 am, but today he has that report to finish first. Rain always makes it worse. Everyone descends on the roads like a plague of locusts on these days, heaven forbid they would wear a raincoat and hold an umbrella for the school run... Zoe starts to shout.

'What's wrong little one?' Cormac asks softly.

'No, no, no, Daddy!' Zoe shouts.

'We won't be long, I promise.'

'No, Daddy!'

Cormac widens his eyes as the traffic lights turn green ahead. He hadn't expected to be so tired all the time, every night was so unpredictable which only made it worse. He gently presses on the accelerator pedal as the traffic starts to move in front of him. Chopin Prelude in D-flat major plays over the radio as he cruises through the mercifully clear roundabout. Progress at last, he thinks. His head feels heavy and he keeps thinking about that report he needs to finish before teaching. His travel mug of coffee rattles and sloshes in its cup holder as he rounds the corner to the nursery carpark opposite his office.

'We're here!' He exclaims, turning to Zoe with a beaming smile. She stares back with her best poker face.

'Let's get you out of here.' Cormac declares and then narrates as he unbuckles Zoe's seatbelt and kisses her on the forehead. She babbles as he lifts her up and holds her on his side. Then, he briskly walks over to the nursery entrance and waits behind another parent in the queue.

Once inside, he tickles her tummy as he takes off her coat. 'What are you going to do today?' He asks her as he takes her hand and they walked into the main room. 'Horsey' she replies as she points to the circle of plastic farm animals on the ground. A crowd of toddling infants are already bumping into each other and playing with them, two are wrestling with each other on the ground over a giraffe. Zoe slows down and holds Cormac's trouser leg.

'It's OK, honey, go on.' Cormac whispers as he ushers her forwards towards a group of little ones encircling one of the carers. Zoe turns to him and tugs his trouser leg again, frantic to climb up. Her bottom lip is starting to quiver, and her eyes are imploring him to hold her.

'Come on little one, look at this' Cormac forces himself to smile and points to the unclaimed horse figurine, it is chestnut brown with black hooves and its forelegs are rearing in an action pose. Zoe tentatively approaches. He catches the eye of one of the carers who has started talking to Zoe and is showing her a zebra. They smile back and he rushes across the room to the exit, turning to wave at Zoe as he leaves. She stares back at him, still frozen in between tears and engagement. The carer picks her up for a cuddle and Cormac walks away, taking a deep breath of the cold autumn air to wake himself up.

Ok, come on! Let's get going, Cormac cajoles himself out of the twisting wrenching feeling in his stomach. The campus beckons and it was now 8.33. Just enough time to finish that report, well, at least a rough draft before heading to class. He nips back to the car, stretches in to get his bag and coffee, an absolute necessity. With each step away from the nursery, he feels his fuzzy, soft fatherhood hat slip from his brow. Time to strap on the worker helmet and head into the breach.

*   *   *

The clock ticks on to 6.35 in the evening, he must leave now, or he will definitely miss Zoe's bedtime. He stifles a yawn and looks over to the empty coffee mug with black coffee stains around the rim, he picks it up and screws on the lid. Papers are strewn across his desk and his computer screen is bursting at the seams with open windows. He clicks the sleep button and grabs his coat and bag. It is already dark outside and the rain from earlier had persisted all day. An earthy smell hits him as he steps out onto the courtyard and he jogs towards the carpark, wilfully ignoring the slops of rainwater that slap against his trouser leg. His silver hatchback is one of the only remaining cars in the carpark and the nursery lights are all off.

He pushes the coffee mug into its slot and turns key in the ignition. He can still feel the invisible straps of his worker helmet cutting into his ears, reminding him of the marking to complete later. Still, he thinks, he's lucky to be able to work from home when he needs to. All told, this was a pretty good gig, and he was making real inroads on that promotion push, too. The head of department had really liked the report, especially the executive summary. It had been a heavy day with six hours of teaching and a departmental meeting in the middle. He had barely had time to eat and he was looking forward to what Jane was going to have ready for them. She does half days on Tuesdays, so she usually rustles up something special for them both.

The journey home is torturous. Standing rainwater bloats over the left lane of the main road squeezing traffic into a crawling snake. The clock ticks on to 6.50 and he starts feeling anxious. He hates being this late, especially now that Zoe can say 'Daddy'. He imagines her looking at the door and pointing. Another red light, precious seconds slip away. He starts calling Jane on the car phone.

'Where are you?' She asks before he has a chance to speak.

'I'm on my way, traffic's a nightmare. I'm not at the high street yet.' Cormac announces. He can hear Zoe shouting and wailing in the background alongside the ending music of 'In the Night Garden'.

'You're not going to make it in time. I'm taking her up, she's getting over-tired and she needs a bath tonight.'

'I'm going as quickly as I can.'

'I've got to go.' She hangs up before he can reply, and he hits another red light.

He pulls into the drive at 7.15. He fumbles with his keys and drops them in the gravel by the front door. Cursing, he grabs them and enters the house. He pulls off his shoes and flings them against the foot of the radiator. Then he runs up the stairs taking two at a time. He is breathless as he gets to the top where he sees Jane waiting for him outside Zoe's room. Her door is ajar but mostly closed and there isn't a noise coming from inside.

'She's asleep. It took me a while to settle her, but she was exhausted. Must have had a busy day at nursery. She was asking for you when I picked her up and kept saying horsey.'

Cormac grits his teeth and gently pushes at the door. The darkness of the room is overwhelming, he peers and blinks to force his vision to adjust. He sees her shadowy form curled up on her side amongst her teddies. She is breathing calmly. He turns back and looks at Jane.

'Sorry.' He says.

'Let's have some dinner.' She replies.

'I've got more marking to do later'.

'I know.' She replies flatly.

Narrator's Impressions of Cormac

When piecing together the fragments of Cormac's pre-pandemic experiences, I was struck by the tension between parental caregiving and occupational commitment. This tension was particularly acute for many fathers in the data who were still rooted in the 'transitional/hybrid' phase of equality parenthood (Hochschild & Machung, 2012). Cormac represents two conflicting pull factors; firstly, the emerging pull to be involved in caregiving for their families, and secondly the stronger pull they felt to maintain a worker/provider identity. Many pre-pandemic fathers wanted to maintain a metaphorical barrier between work and family time, this typically aligned with patriarchal, structural patterns of men as 9 till 5 workers and evening and weekend carers. Although the fathers in this data set were co-parenting with highly educated, professional women, the anticipated 'downshifting' (Gatrell, 2005, p. 135) of their work commitment was almost universally neglected, despite many fathers having a viable option to do so. This aligns with evidence from caring masculinity research, which persistently found alignment between the traditional 'breadwinner' role and fathers' construction of their work identity (Hanlon, 2012; Lee & Lee, 2018).

Organisations were also complicit in the reinforced idealisation of 'career-oriented, instrumental males working very hard for the business' (Alvesson & Due Billing, 2009, p. 9). Here the parallel actions of ideological patriarchy supersede rising desires many men felt to become more involved parents. During this period, organisations acted as major constraining influences on men's sense of freedom to do the physical and emotionally involved caregiving for their families, even when they wanted to do so (Kelland et al., 2022; Murgia & Poggio, 2013). Many still felt hailed as subjects of the enduring patriarchal structure of organisational reality, tempted by promotions and status-linked prestige to fulfil their provider status in lieu of caregiving responsibilities. It was only in the aftermath of the pandemics during which working fathers had lived the daily reality of home-working and caregiving that the blurred lines between work and family life became the catalyst for a re-ordering of the 'gender regime' (Acker, 2006) at home and in organisations. This reordering was a crucial phase that redirected organisations away from valuing sex differences (Irigaray & Gill, 1993) and utopian ideals of women's unique motherhood qualities (Perkins Gilman, 1915). Instead, the narrative shifted towards recognising and valuing equitable roles for parents and enhanced responsibility for men as caregivers equally capable of caring for their children.

Andrea Doucet (2006a, b) described two feminist perspectives relevant to this debate concerning parent's caregiving roles and responsibilities: 'difference feminism' and 'equality feminism'. These two theoretical perspectives provide contrasting insights into how parents at work can be arranged and valued within organisational experiences. Irigaray highlights the irreducibility of certain aspects of the woman's experience as one basis for valuing and asserting the identity of woman as 'different' to man and therefore constructed as distinct in social relations. There are problematic aspects to this view of essentialist feminist theorising in the context of trans rights. Though it is true that women physically go through pregnancy, birth (and recovery) and breastfeeding, there are notable exceptions that highlight the importance of re-evaluating gender difference for parents at work (see 'the dad who gave birth...' Hattenstone, 2019). It is important to state that the physical differences pertaining to pregnancy for women did require differential policies in the post-pandemic era; groups like Maternity Action (2020) led the way with their proposal for an equitable 6+6+6 model of six months protected leave for mothers and fathers and the option to share six months. This model recognised the physical impact of pregnancy, but also valued the vital role of fathers. Physical differences should not provide an enduring differential basis for gender-based differentiation. As Doucet described, equality feminism promoted equal involvement for men and women in domestic, and hands-on, caregiving (Andrea Doucet, 2006a, b, p. 23) and this was the transformative shift that helped to reconstruct gender norms for parents at work.

For Cormac, the 'providing for' role (Jordan, 2020, p. 23) was still superior in his approximation of what fathers' parental roles should be and 'a core part of being masculine' (Connell, 2005), which reproduced the traditional breadwinner norms of western hegemonic masculinity. Cormac answered the organisational 'hail' as an ideal worker, despite his desire to be more involved, placing him in a hybrid masculinity (Bridges & Pascoe, 2014; Randles, 2018) limbo. His symbolic interpellation to organisational norms diminished his opportunities to engage in daily act of care to a subordinate position. It was only when organisations and states responded to overwhelming post-pandemic demands to equally value fathers' and mothers' caregiving, that the vanguard of organisational parental leave changes (Brearley, 2021; Fatherhood Institute, 2022; Maternity Action, 2020) could proliferate. The move to provide equal parental leave for fathers gave men the permission to embody new formations of 'caring masculinities' (Elliott, 2016; Jordan, 2020; Lee & Lee, 2018) that can 'reject domination' by valuing 'positive emotion, interdependence, and relationality' (Elliott, 2016, p. 241). It was this realignment of the valued attributes of masculinities that enabled men to dislocate their masculine identity from breadwinning, but during the PPE, this was still a pipedream.

The data showed disparate approaches to how fathers allocated their time between work and family, which reflected ongoing debates during the PPE (Crespi & Ruspini, 2015; Hojgaard, 1997; Huffman et al., 2014; Hunter et al., 2017; Kangas et al., 2019; Kaufman, 2018). Some fathers described their strict, delineated approach to work and family time as distinct activities and attributed equal importance to both through their time and energy commitments. However, other fathers were more inclined to prioritise their work commitments as both intrinsically important to their identity and as emblematic of their provider role. Such variance exists within a host of sociological studies during the PPE of 'working parents' research from 1989 to 2020 (Bailey, 2015; Brandth & Kvande, 2018; Burgess, 1998; Chesley, 2011; Collier, 2019; Gatrell, 2005; Hochschild & Machung, 2012). From traditional breadwinner roles, to 'transitional' hybrid roles, to the rare egalitarian mode (Hochschild & Machung, 2012), Cormac represents the inherent tensions fathers navigated in balancing oft-conflicting societal expectations.

The socially constructed worker and father ideals sustained complex tensions between protector/provider fatherhood and the progressive ideals of equal parenthood (Jordan, 2020). These tensions ran parallel to a breadth of academic discourse debating egalitarian ideals for the modern father in UK and European contexts (Burgess, 1998; A. Doucet, 2006a, b; Gatto, 2020; Goldstein-Gidoni, 2020; Kvande & Brandth, 2019; Peukert, 2017; Wall & Arnold, 2007). This ambivalent discourse echoed the ideological conflict within studies of men and masculinities regarding the enduring 'patriarchal dividend' (Connell, 2005) and the 'patriarchal deficit' (Bailey, 2015). The 'patriarchal dividend' also related to the problematic hegemonic appropriation of caring attitudes and behaviour, which Demetriou (2001) described as 'dialectical pragmatism' reconstructing a 'hybrid hegemonic masculinity' (Demetriou, 2001; Messerschmidt, 2018). The myth of 'new fathers' (Messner, 1993) having their cake and eating it remained problematic throughout the post-pandemic epoch and maintained tensions in constructions of 'involved fatherhood' (Kimmel et al., 2005; Messner, 1993; Miller, 2011). These discourses exist alongside media debates of the representation of fathers (Hunter et al., 2017; Kangas et al., 2019), which often reduced fatherhood to gender-role binaries and reinforced gendered assumptions.

When we consider terms such as 'involved fatherhood' today, we may find ourselves dismissive of such explicitly illogical pre-pandemic denials of the vital role of caregiving fathers. Even at the time, evidence was mounting of the transformative effect of equally involved fathers in the nurturing of children as a societal imperative that has positive outcomes for women's equal engagement in the workplace too (Norman, 2020; Norman et al., 2014). Sadly, for expectant fathers, these narratives were still obscured by normalised language of father's secondary role as caregivers.

ALFRED

Alfred opens a new email window in Outlook. He sits forward, shunting his chair closer to his desk. His back arches and his shoulders hunch as he suspends his fingers over the keyboard like a concert pianist about to begin.

> Date: 24 May 2019
> To: Human Resources
> Subject: Paternity Leave.
> Hello
> My wife is due to give birth on July 28th, 2019, and I would like to take some paternity leave. Please can you advise what I'm entitled to?
> Thanks
> Alfred

Alfred leans back and exhales. A weight has been lifted, at least for now. He looks around the office, his bookshelves are still sparsely populated with his printed thesis and a couple of textbooks his supervisor gave to him. He's just finished his final teaching session for the year, he is shattered. He's ready for the weekend and a sip of non-alcoholic beer in solidarity with Katherine's pregnancy restrictions. It's the first couples' antenatal class next week and he hasn't read the literature Katherine sent to him yet. He chews his thumbnail and tears off a strip. *Time for some lunch and a coffee*, he thinks as he stands up, stretches, and strides out of the room.

Waiting in the queue for the hot meals, the smell of fried fish, chips, salt, and vinegar makes him salivate. He looks down at his tummy, it's bigger than he would like to be. At the end of the island there is a punnet of baked potatoes. He reluctantly pulls himself away from the glistening, crispy batter and bypasses the queue to serve himself.

'Hi, Alfred' A woman's voice hails him from over his shoulder.

Alfred turns around, 'Oh! Hi, Sue. How are you?'

'Good thanks, how's Katherine doing?'

'Yeah, good thanks. Still feeling rough at times, but she's doing well. She goes on mat leave next week.'

'Really?'

'Yeah, doctor's orders, and mine!'

'Is she OK?'

'Yeah, she's fine, baby's fine, too. She has preeclampsia, though, so she needs to take it easy. I've told her she has to slow down once she's off. No more work for a while, that's *my* role now.'

'You need to take good care of her, Alfred. Lots of pampering!'

'Yeah, I'll have to stop gaming for a while, I suppose. I've been doing more cooking recently, but I burned the potatoes last night.'

'I'm sure they were still lovely!' She says with a mock smile. 'But seriously, my Davy was a rock for me when our two were born. I wouldn't have coped without him cleaning and helping with night feeds. He really stepped up. I think fatherhood brings out the best in men, don't you?'

'Yeah, I guess so… Hopefully!' Alfred chuckles. 'I had been considering reducing my hours, you know? I even thought about shared parental leave, especially with Katherine's job paying more than mine. I like the idea of spending some quality time with the baby every week, too, but Katherine's health has made me rethink. She's been so stressed out with it all and I can't see that getting any easier when she has to return to work. I want to take the pressure off her and it's important that she has this time, isn't it?'

'Yes, of course. What did you have in mind, though?'

'I was thinking of going down to four days a week.'

'Oh, don't bother. Fewer hours, less pay, and same amount of work. Take it from me, you are better staying full time.'

'Yeah, that's what others have said. Well, anyway, if I want to make sure Katherine can choose how much *she* works and that means going for a promotion.'

'You applying this year, then? You should!'

'Yeah, I think so. Not sure if I'm ready, but it seems like the right option.'

'No time like the present, especially with a baby coming. Pop by my office and I'll help you out.' Sue beams at him and looks down at his plate. 'So, baked potato and salad, aye? Healthy choice!'

'Suppose so' He looks down at the drab, dry salad leaves and meagre three cherry tomatoes rolling at the lip of his plate. The small polystyrene tub of tuna looks equally underwhelming... 'I'm trying to lose some weight... you know, for when the baby comes.'

'Good for you. Trust me, you'll pile it all back on once they arrive. You need the carbs with all the sleepless nights!' Sue chuckles and selects a baked potato for herself.

'So, how's your little one? ...' Alfred hesitates, searching for the name.

'Rose? Oh, she's really good thanks, loving nursery. We're going to Centre Parks after the marking's done and we can't wait. You'll love family life, Alfred!'

'How old is she now?' Alfred replies. He notices two women, one older than the other, and baby entering the seating area. He watches as they search for a seat. He can hear the mewling cries of the baby.

'She turns three in June, time flies.' Sue says. Alfred doesn't reply, he is still looking at the women and the baby. 'Anyway, must dash as am eating this at my desk while I do email. Good seeing you!' Sue waves her hand across his field of vision and he auto smiles as Sue heads over to the counter.

Alfred stands in the serving area and contemplates buying a banana too, while continuing to watch the women with the baby. The seconds stretch out into minutes and he feels a tap on his shoulder.

'Can I help you with anything?' An older woman with a warm smile says. She's wearing the black uniform and cap of the refectory staff.

'Sorry, I was miles away. I'm ready to pay now.' Alfred says as he selects the banana from the nearby bowl.

'They'll be OK.' The woman says, as she looks over to the women and baby. 'Women always manage.'

'Yeah.' Alfred replies. 'They do, I suppose.'

Alfred pays for his lunch and finds an empty table nearby. The hubbub of the cafeteria surrounds him like a swarm of bees. He starts eating this baked potato, it is barely warm, and the salad is tasteless. He takes out his phone, opens his email and scrolls down to the latest email from Katherine from earlier this week titled 'top tips for new dads.' It's still unopened. He taps the attachment and looks at the PDF document: *tip one—Be there for your partner, tip two—It's OK to cry, tip three—be prepared!* ... Alfred stops reading and puts down the phone. He knows he is expected to cry when the baby arrives, he's even talked to Katherine about it, but he doesn't feel anything right now. He wants to feel something, he really does. He watched 'One Born Every Minute' with Katherine a couple of weekends ago and felt nothing. 'It'll come' she'd said to him, but all he could think of was the worry about sleep loss. He really can't afford to be off his game next academic year, not with promotions coming up. As for being prepared, he knows he *has* to step up. He stands up and takes his half-eaten lunch plate over to the rack.

*   *   *

Writing parents at work is writing sleep.
It's writing sleeplessness, restlessness,
Barely consciousness.
It's writing no sleep,
Co-sleep, stop and go sleep.
I don't know sleep.
It's writing sleep training,
Complaining,
Relationship straining.
It's writing sleep dread,
GO TO BED!
It's writing midnight wake,
Tomorrow's fake
Wakefulness performance.
It's writing caffeine, please.
It's writing, get on,
It's writing, pretend… survive.

*   *   *

Alfred sits opposite a health visitor who is dressed in smart, casual trousers, and a jacket. She is holding a clipboard and a pen and nodding along as she takes notes from the description of family life that his pregnant wife is offering. She turns to Alfred and he smiles back at her.

'What about you, Alfred. What does *being* a father look like for you?'

'I want to be honest with you about this and I've spoken with Katherine about this before. I know what I don't want to be and that's like my dad.

He was always at work, golf on the weekends, just had no time for me at all. It's different now, we can chat about things, but nothing too deep. That makes him uncomfortable. Well, I don't want that. I want to be more involved, you know?'

'Yes, of course. Go on...' The health visitor smiles.

'It's not that I think my dad got everything wrong. He provided for us and we never went hungry. He protected us and I think that's important for a man to do for his family.'

'Yes, and what does *providing* mean to you?'

'It's very important to me, you know. It's not just being the provider, it's what my work means to me...' Alfred pauses and look over to Katherine. She is sitting forward on their sofa and focused on him.

'I got a promotion recently and my works means a hell of a lot to me, it's part of my identity as a man and as a father. This promotion means I can give Katherine the flexibility to choose her hours. I want to be there for my kids and to listen to them and hug them and bathe them and read to them and everything, you know? But I also need to make the money so we can have a lovely life together.'

'Yes, of course' The health visitor replies while scribbling some notes.

'But it's just hard. I want to be my best self when I'm doing this. I feel a sense of duty to protect my family, but I also feel the guilt that I won't be able to be present all the time.'

'Thanks Alfred, I think I have what I need. Back to you, Katherine, how is your mental state, how prepared do you feel?'

Alfred sits back and crosses his arms, while Katherine talks. He listens to what she has to say and tries to push his uncertainty down. I need to be strong for them now, he thinks.

Narrators Reflections on Alfred

The expectations that underpinned Alfred's ideas and decisions about fatherhood reflect the transitional fatherhood attitudes of this period (Hochschild & Machung, 2012) whereby some men who wanted to be more involved found it difficult to let go of the breadwinner or career identity (Bach, 2019; Chesley, 2011; Reid, 2018). Of course, there were significant structural and societal barriers to this, not least the gender pay gap, which described endemic privileging and 'patriarchal dividend' (Connell, 2005) afforded to men's careers at the expense of women's. Indeed, evidence from this time showed that fathers who maintained traditional breadwinner identities gained most from the patriarchal dividend (Berdahl & Moon, 2013). This was particularly the case for expectant father's whose career trajectories came into focus through social discourse with their peers. These conversations exposed an interpellation process whereby expectant fathers were 'hailed' by their peers as patriarchal subjects and worthy recipients of career advancement during their preparations for parenthood. Seemingly, greater career responsibility and renumeration went hand in hand with social constructions of fatherhood for some of these men. Such hailing symbolised cultural discourse that reinforced the sex-role of men as providers within wider society.

One problematic issue that resulted from the expectation of patriarchal fatherhood was the suppression of men's mental health in common discourse. Alfred squashed his emotional response to becoming a father and this reflected the sense of marginalisation these expectant fathers felt in the process of 'becoming' a father. This normative discourse presupposed that fathers were in control of their emotions and represented a secondary role in the construction of emotional security for new families. Of course, history has taught us that this 'patriarchal deficit' (Bailey, 2015; Gatto, 2020; Kelland et al., 2022) was particularly damaging to the feminist equality project, which did not fully realise the transition to equal parenting until father's involvement in care was equally valued and provided for (Brandth & Kvande, 2019; Kvande & Brandth, 2019).

Fathers today embrace their role as 'attentive, responsible, competent, and responsive' (Tronto, 2015) equal members of society who 'care with' their partners. However, this was not always the case for the post-pandemic epoch as many fathers espoused culturally normalised caring rhetoric while succumbing to ongoing complicity with patriarchal ideology in a hybridised reproduction of hegemonic masculinity (Bridges & Pascoe, 2014; Demetriou, 2001; Messerschmidt, 2018; Palmer, 2021). We now know that it was the inadequate organisational and state provision for men's caregiving that restricted the caregiving potential of these fathers. Many genuinely did care about their role as involved fathers but could not balance the financial damage and economic necessity of their provider role with their desire to be more heavily involved. Without the economic mandate provided through extended, full pay parental leave for all parents, fathers choices were constrained; this defined their capacity to care equally with the typical primary caregivers in the PPE, women.

JULIAN

Julian rubs her temples and scrunches her eyelids together to reset her blurring vision. Her shoulder-length hair is pinned back with clips and her suit jacket is creasing against the armrests of her faux leather office chair. She has read and reread the paragraph on her computer screen, but the words just wouldn't sink in. *You need degrees in mathematics and law to decipher this,* she thought. What would it cost if she split the leave 50/50, or 60/40, or 75/25 with Theo? She highlighted a passage:

> You need to share the pay and leave in the first year after your child is born or placed with your family.[1]

She wanted to exclusively breastfeed for at least six months, *maybe he could take over after that*, she thought. She had already talked about it with Theo. He had initially seemed enthusiastic about taking some time out, though he kept mentioning that he couldn't breastfeed, which had felt like code for not wanting to actually take any leave. She suspected he was saying what she wanted to hear, but she hadn't confronted him on that, yet. They had read the guidance document together last week and Theo said he was happy with whatever she decided, which was making her feel guilty. He was so busy at work at the moment, and his career was taking off. It was the happiest she had seen him in a long time, he was really excited to be a dad and kept taking about his role to provide for his family, especially after he had been offered that promotion. She wanted him to be happy.

A gust of cold air blows in from the open window and sends a shiver down her spine. She reaches backwards and pulls on her jacket from the backrest of her chair before walking over to the window to close it. It is just her in the office, but she knows Gary must have been in earlier as his lunchbox, replete with apple core and banana skin, is still on his desk. It's usually Gary who opens the window, too. She feels a wave of nausea after she locks the frame shut and rests her forehead on the cooling surface of the windowpane to distract herself. After a few seconds, she looks down at the courtyard below and the students entering and leaving the building. It's halfway through semester two and she knows the timing of her pregnancy could have been better, especially the due date being in May.

---

[1] https://www.gov.uk/shared-parental-leave-and-pay

She wanted to compensate for this by finding the best return to work date
and thought January might work well. She had built her profile over the
last five years as the programme leader and her research was going great,
but she can't shake the niggling fear that she will be left behind if she
doesn't stay in touch over the coming months.

She hears the office door latch click and turns to see her colleague,
Gary, enter the room. He's wearing sandy coloured chinos, brown
brogues, and a tailored pastel blue shirt. As he closes the door, she can
smell his cologne cloud as it diffuses around the room. She contemplates
re-opening the window to let it escape but thinks better of it. He smiles
and glances at her display as he passed her desk.

'Shared Parental Leave, huh?' He says, smirking. 'Good luck with that!'
Jenny and I couldn't make head nor tail of that thing. It's so much easier
to just do it the old-fashioned way. It worked best for us anyway.' He
lowered himself slowly into his chair and clicked his mouse to awaken the
screen. 'How have I got 30 emails since lunchtime?'

'Same way I got 35.' Julian replies. Her nausea is still lingering so she
heads back to her desk, opens the drawer, and picks an oatcake from the
half-finished packet.

'You need to learn to say no to most of them, you know.'

'Easier said than done.'

'It gets easier every time you do it.' Gary says, smiling as he emphatically
clicks his mouse. 'What are you and Theo thinking of doing then?'

'We are still deciding, but I'll probably take it all.' Julian replies. 'You're
right, it's much easier that way.'

'Yeah, it worked out fine for us. Jenny's back at work part time and
she's really happy with how it went.'

'That's good.'

'Yeah'

'Can I ask you a question?' Julian asks, taking the last few bites of her
oatcake and a sip of water.

'Sure.' Gary stops typing and looks up from his screen.

'As a father, did you feel like you missed out in the first year?'

'Wow...Hmm...' Gary chuckles and turns in his swivel chair to face
Julian. 'That's a difficult question... Did I miss out?' He pauses, looks
upwards at the box panel ceiling and laces his fingers back and forth. The
silence grows and Julian feels the urge to speak.

'It's just...' She starts.

'I love being a dad and love spending time with Ellie.' He blurts, still looking up at the ceiling. 'It just wasn't *practical* to take a big chunk of time when Ellie was born. I'd just got that promotion and, you know, grant proposals and papers in progress' He looks down from the ceiling and faces her, 'I just couldn't pause that stuff. Do you know what I mean?'

'Yeah. Sure, makes sense.' Julian replies.

'It's not that I didn't want to take more time. I suppose I just like it more now Ellie is talking and asking questions and we can *do* more together. I feel like I can really get to know her as a person. Do you know what I mean?' If I could have taken a few weeks in the second half, or even better, now… Well, that would really make me stop and think, you know. It was the whole sharing thing, it felt like a big commitment and the money side, you know.' He stares at Julian expectantly and waits for her to reply.

Julian smiles and autoreplies, 'sure' as she scrolls up to the section on 'eligibility' she reread this morning to confirm that Gary could in fact have done exactly what he has just described. She thinks better of sharing this with him and instead closes the window and re-opens her emails.

'I'm sure you'll work it out' Gary states as he turns back to his screen too.

Another cluster of new emails appear on her screen and bump the others down her list. Her back and her hips are starting to ache. She can't face them right now; it's getting late and she wants to beat the traffic home. *I'll do these later this evening,* she thinks.

*   *   *

Julian exits the lift and see's Toby walking over from the stairwell to her. She's wearing a light grey suit, black shoes, and white blouse.

'Fancy a decaf?' Toby calls over.

'Yeah, definitely, but I've only got half an hour until class.'

'That works for me.' Toby says. 'How's the sickness? Mine was awful in the first trimester. Not too bad in the third, thankfully.'

'It keeps coming in waves. It's my hips and ankles that are killing me now and I can't get through a class without needing the loo.'

'Yeah, it's a magical time!' Toby laughs.

They find a quiet table away from the students.

'So, how did it go?' Toby asks.

'With Pete?'

'Yeah'

'Not as well as I'd hoped.'

'Oh... Why? Did you mention what I told you about my arrangement?'

'Yeah, I explained exactly how you spread your annual leave over the year.'

'You shared my work schedule with him?'

Yes, thanks again for that. He just kept saying, *show me where that is written in the policy.* I said it was a local arrangement, which *was* in the policy, but he wasn't having it. He told me to check with HR!'

'This place is ridiculous! We're just numbers on a spreadsheet to them. Have you spoken to the union about it?'

'No, no... I, I, I just don't want to rock the boat at this stage, you know.'

'Did you check with HR?'

'Yes.' Julian says, pulling an exaggerated glum face.

'Oh Gawd.'

'Their reply was, *Oh, that's a local arrangement.* I could have screamed! It's either a policy or it's not!' Julian sits back in her chair and sighs.

*   *   *

Toby had also offered Julian some 2nd hand baby clothes, which was really kind. She has two children and seems to know everything about every parent in the department. It was like it was her mission to coordinate everyone and learn their stories. Julian liked the idea of this group of parents finding common ground beyond the trials and tribulations of redrafting her latest article or meeting a book chapter deadline. She looked around her office at the array of academic iconography, from her bound PhD thesis to the growing pile of theory books she had yet to properly arrange on the shelf, her old identity was about to morph into something different.

The Narrator's Impressions of Julian

Julian's story highlights the often-oppressive workplace cultural attitudes that working women faced when expecting a baby. This is especially true of women who attempt to integrate their careers with their expected social role as a primary caregiving mother (Berdahl & Moon, 2013). Evidence from this time also highlighted that women were often mistreated if they chose not to have children (Berdahl & Moon, 2013; Eagly & Karau, 2002; Gloor et al., 2018). Julian was a difficult character to reconstruct because her story reveals a troubling picture of the pressure women felt to conform to a secondary role within masculine organisational norms and their presumptive 'social role' as nurturant mother as a complementary figure to the male committed worker (Eagly et al., 2000). Such gender-based social role pressure feeds into the 'difference feminism' construction of how 'feminine' attributes of care, empathy and relatedness should be separately valued for working mothers, rather than being integrated and valued within progressive formulations of caring masculinities (Elliott, 2016). Julian's acceptance of her role as primary caregiver was present in more than one example in the data fragments and is indicative of the persistent and influence of patriarchal norms and marketised work intensification within higher education (Acker & Armenti, 2004; Acker & Dillabough, 2007; Gill, 2009). Such norms were incompatible with what we now view as a human right to a fair balance of work and family life without detriment.

Nowhere was the ideological pressure of patriarchal organisational norms felt more acutely than with Julian's transition from being a 'workhorse' to having to embrace saying 'no'. This symbolic moment of identity shift signalled the end of the ideal worker lie in which women could 'have it all' as equals to men. The cold, hard reality for the expectant mother was the realisation of their own induction into the constraining reality of the motherhood penalty (Budig & England, 2001; Cahusac & Kanji, 2014; Horne & Breitkreuz, 2018). This penalty is not only financial, but also symbolises a cumulative physical and emotional burden by virtue of the second shift of domestic labour predominantly falling on primary caregiver mother (Hochschild, 1997; Hochschild & Machung, 2012). When women agreed to take the majority of parental leave, they also symbolically agreed to shoulder much of the associated domestic responsibilities heading into the future. As we know, such decisions were detrimental to women's careers and contrasting quantitative evidence from the time proved that mothers whose partners instead worked reduced hours in the first year of their child's life had a positive association with mothers' career advancement three years later (Norman, 2020; Norman et al., 2014).

Crucial to Julian's story is the intervention of other experienced parents who intervened to share their experiences and advise her of ways to navigate their new life as a parent at work. However, we also gain insights into the inconsistencies experienced by expectant parents when attempting to apply this advice. The problem of unreliable gatekeepers with discretionary power is again highlighted as an unfair cultural barrier to some women's access to enhanced parental experiences. At its worst, inconsistent managerial interactions with expectant mothers led to women being 'pushed out' of organisations (Cahusac & Kanji, 2014), but the commonplace masculine, rule-bound, performative culture also led to some expectant mothers suffering the binary conflict of motherhood versus career success (Acker & Dillabough, 2007), which was exacerbated by gatekeeper line managers who had less flexible attitudes to work-family life. These immovable gatekeeper barriers, inherent in the fabric of organisational life, formed the grounding for necessary resistance and subversion. As we all sit today, securely in our bubbles, it is hard to imagine one individual having such power over our rights, but we should never forget it was the collectively reasserted voice of parents at work in the post-pandemic era that shifted the narrative towards truly flexible working today.

This final story provides some evidence of the winds of change that were beginning to blow during the PPE. Though these subversive acts may seem relatively minor by contemporary standards, they were the important first steps towards subversion of the masculinised organisational norm I have outlined today.

MAYDAY PART 2: FROM INTENTION TO ACTION

Writing parents at work is writing relationships.
It's writing from shared experiences that make
Work workable and unworkable.
It's relying on your family to make family life liveable.
It's community.
It's solidarity.
It's care.
It's resistance and
Subversion.

Cormac wanders along a dimly lit, turquoise corridor lined with monotonous pine office doors and frosted glass walls. He glances in through each of the exposed window panel strips and sneaks an opportune peak though the cracked doorways of some more inviting rooms as he passes by, though he does not linger for long enough to initiate contact. He carries an overfilled his mug of tea, adorned with the university branding.

Small slops breach the lip of the mug as he walks along and a sporadic trail of splashes land on the carpet in his wake. He pauses and stands outside the neighbouring office to his. Inhaling the rising steam from his mug, he takes a tentative slurp of the scalding liquid and looks down the corridor. He wants to extend the liminal time between work and refreshment. If he goes inside his office, he can't kid himself that he is using necessary time to get a drink. The window at the end of the corridor beckons him for a pensive moment of reflective staring, but he is interrupted before can make his move.

'Hey, Cormac. Let's see the latest piccies then!' A voice hails him from inside the adjoining office.

Cormac gulps down a scorching mouthful and feels it scratch his throat. 'Hey', he rasps in reply stepping into the doorway of the open office. He leans on the steel doorframe and warms his hands on the outside of his mug as further whisps of vapourised tea rise like light seeking sapling tendrils to caress his cheek. A table in the middle of the room is decorated with blue and red union fliers and an oversized rainbow banner drapes over it, touching the floor on one side. His colleague, Mary perches on the edge of her seat and turns to look directly at him. The view through the window to the outside world is obscured by a billowing fog escaping upwards into the sky, presumably from a nearby vent.

'You never share pics on the network.' Mary says with a faux grumpy face.

'I don't like to share their pictures too widely, privacy you know.'

'Of course, of course. I'm just ribbing you!' Mary replies. She is wearing a flowery blouse, purple suit trousers and silver lined trainers which she waggles from side to side as she talks. 'Sooo, where's the latest pics?'

Cormac rummages in his pocket and pulls out his smartphone. He clears a series of alerts that have accumulated since he last opened the case. Scrolling past some recent pictures of Zac in the bath with Zoe, he finds one his wife took of all four of them together, on a nature walk they recently did, the sun had deigned to grace them with its presence that day and they are beaming at the camera. It's an idyllic picture, like the ones you see in countryside themed magazines. He shows Mary, handing her the phone and standing alongside her.

'Aww, that's lovely, Cormac. Gosh, he's really grown since I last saw him.'

'Yeah, he's growing fast.'

'How old is he now?'

'Just turned 4, he goes to school in September.'

'What about Zoe, is she one yet?'

'13 months now, she's almost walking.'

'Jeez! That's ridiculous! I remember when you brought her in for the first time after you went on parental leave.'

'Yeah, that was a funny day. It was only the second time I had been out with her without Jane. I was really nervous. I was so worried she would start crying for her mum and I would have to take her into Jane's work, but it went OK, didn't it? It's funny thinking about that now. I was so scared, more scared than I think I had ever been before.'

'Well, you didn't show it, you were a natural.' Mary says, turning back to her screen and clicking her mouse to open a document. 'So, did you see the group discussion this morning? I've been drafting this with Toby and think it's ready for another pair of eyes.'

'Yeah, I saw your message. Was going to reply later.'

'We need your voice in this, Cormac. You're one of the few fathers I know of in this place who has ever spoken up about shared parental leave. It can't just be the mums with this claim. If they know that this represents the whole network, they are going to have to listen to it!'

'I know, I know.' Cormac replies as he starts to scan the document on Mary's screen.

'Did you see the first draft?'

'Yes, I saw it last week. I was discussing it with Alfred. His partner's expecting their first in few months' time. They're facing the same barriers we faced, the numbers just don't add up for them. We need to be more ambitious.'

'That's what I was just saying to Toby! I have started drafting something else' Mary says while gesturing to an A4 pad on her desk with a list of bullet points. She points to the nearby vacant swivel chair and Cormac pulls it up to the desk. Outside the room, Julian waves at them both and takes a rest against the doorframe. She is holding her lower back with one hand and carrying a flask mug in the other. She is wearing blue corduroy dungarees, a white, long-sleeved top, and white trainers.

'Just going for a walk. How are you both?' Julian asks.

'Hey, come in, come in, we need your thoughts on this, too.' Mary calls over to Julian whose cheeks are flushed. Her hair is tied back exposing reddened eyelids and mottled brow. She slowly enters the room.

'Please, take this seat.' Cormac says as stands up.

'Take mine! You, keep reading!' Mary chuckles and stand up. She grabs her notepad in one hand and takes Toby's free hand to guide her to the chair.

'I can't stay long.' Julian says as she lowers herself onto the seat. She unscrews the mug lid and releases peppermint vapour into the room.

'You OK?' Mary asks.

'Yeah, just finding these final few weeks harder and harder. It's not slowing down, it's like they expect all the projects to be tied up in a neat bow. I miss coffee too.' She laughs along with Mary and Cormac.

'That's why I want to speak to you, though unfortunately not to solve the coffee situation. We need to include more voices like yours to reflect the experiences of pregnant women in this claim. We want to show them what it's really like to be pregnant in this place.'

'Yeah.' Julian replies. She takes another sip from her mug and takes a deep breath. 'It's a bit shit right now.' Julian replies with a forced chuckle.

'Trust me, I've been there.' Mary places her hand on Julian's arm and inclines her head.

'It's the difference between the supportive words and the lack of action that gets to me most. For example, I haven't had a risk assessment yet and it's almost time for me to go on leave. Also, it might seem silly, but I asked about not doing 3-hour seminars this semester, they said it wouldn't happen, but guess what appeared on my timetable? Once it was there, there was no way to remove it! I'm absolutely shattered by the end of hour two so god only knows what the students think of the final hour…'

'What did your line manager say about the risk assessment?' Cormac asks.

'I'm too embarrassed to ask them about it now. I feel like it's my fault.'

'It's not!' Mary states. 'How long is it now until you are off?'

'Three weeks. I'm literally counting down the days. It sounds awful, but I'm really ready for the break. I know it's going to be exhausting in a different way, but I need to get away from *this* for a while. My current life just doesn't fit inside these walls.'

'I know. I felt the same way. Still do a lot of the times, sorry to say.' Mary replies.

Cormac stands alongside Mary and re-reads the text on Mary's screen. He drains the last mouthful of his tea and breathes out the hot air. The message is right, but something *is* missing, it's too *safe he thinks to himself.*

'We're still playing by their rules, their hierarchy.' he mutters.

'Yes! Exactly! What I really want to do is organise a group of parents to camp outside the CEOs office and let our children loose to bang on the door demanding to be heard. They'll struggle to mothball that response so quickly.' Mary replies

'It's the urgency that's lacking.' Julian says as she gets to her feet. 'It's too easy for them to push these issues down the road and months become years, years become decades...meanwhile more people will go through what I'm experiencing right now.'

'It's just more of the same old shit, isn't it? How many more exploited pregnancies are we going to tolerate on the altar of productivity and progress before we draw a line in the sand? We need to show them we won't accept these norms any longer!' Cormac declares.

'Yes!' Mary replies with a wide grin, her fingers rhythmically rap on a bullet point list on her A4 pad.

'They need to know we exist as a collective, that we aren't going away, that we stand in solidarity as one movement, and that we are here to demand change, now! We can't keep flexing our lives to their rigid rules. I want them to see the other side of our lived experiences, to show them what being a parent at work means. We are going to show them what flexibility should be about by bringing our children into the workplace when our timetables clash with childcare. I am not going to call in any more favours from family and friends. It's time to push the emotional and physical burden back onto their shoulders.'

'Read this.' Mary says as she places her notepad onto the desk between them.

Cormac and Julian both read the bullet list, their heads both nod enthusiastically as they scan down the page. Cormac's foot starts to tap on the ground.

There is silence in the room, but Mary is smiling.

'This is it, Mary!' Cormac exclaims. 'I am going to write to the fathers in the network today. We need to start acting as one. We're going to start the clock on this change. It has to come from all of us.' Cormac bangs down his mug in a mock emphatic gesture and a small chip of ceramic pings off from the bottom edge, sliding across the table surface.

'No time like the present!' Mary replies picking up the chip and throwing it in her deskside bin. She opens the network homepage and a new conversation box. 'Let's write it together. This can be a moment of fellowship at the start of our journey. Julian wheels her chair closer to the screen and Cormac leans in. Mary starts to type (Image 3.2).

The time has come for us to act, will you join us?...

Image 3.2   'The Spirit of Subversion' by Rachel Hunter (2021)

Narrators Reflections on Mayday: Part 2—From Intentions to Action

Friends, the second story of Mayday represents the vital role of collective action in the transition from patriarchal organisational norms to equitable, caring working practices for all. In the spirit of people-centred organisational praxis (Freire, 2004, 2017; Horton et al., 1990), these parents first came together to express and articulate their individual experiences of workplace oppression. It was through this shared experience that they began to reflect on their occasional complicity in their own oppression (Althusser, 2014; Freire, 2017). Through that praxis, they gained the collective purpose to act to create a new, long term, democratic vision for their working lives. The first step was solidarity and mutual support. The 'Mayday' spirit of subversion grew from shared experiences of parental inequity and a recognition of their shared oppressor, embodied in this story by Marley. Throughout the data samples I uncovered, it was clear that these parents not only knew but held deeply critical views of the masculinised organisation. It was only when their individual voices found a platform that they started to make change.

The role of masculinities in this narrative cannot be underplayed and it was the embodied caregiving experiences of fathers that transformed men from hybridised rhetorical allies (Demetriou, 2001; Messerschmidt, 2018) to genuinely progressive, allegiant comrades. The vision of our contemporary 'caring masculinities' was borne from the 'rejection of domination and [the] integration of values of care, such as positive emotion, interdependence, and relationality' (Elliott, 2016, p. 241). This vision drew on Connell's foundational concept of masculine 're-embodiment' (2005, p. 233) and the 'hands-on' acts of caregiving, which became a template for the necessary experiential learning that affected working father's perceptions of care. Yet this was not a straightforward road to enlightenment. We must not forget how easily the ghosts of hegemonic masculinity in organisations (Acker, 1990, 2006; Burnett et al., 2012) could haunt us again. Patriarchal artefacts still blight us today, even decades after the pandemics. They resurface as masculinised data cyphers (Blackman, 2019) that infected our algorithms with a legacy of gender biases (Zhao et al., 2017). Re-writing the script of masculinities for parents at work was a multifaceted process that involved everyone from institutions to individuals in a new cycle of change from all levels of organisational life. It was not enough to wait for the cycle of reproduction to correct itself; the masculine domination (Bourdieu, 2001) was too endemic and embedded into the idealised breadwinner worker trope (Collier, 2019). It was only when fathers experienced the value of caregiving (Bunting, 2020; A. Doucet, 2006a, b; Tronto, 2015) that they internalised a re-embodied masculinity and joined the collective movement to subvert the patriarchy.

This final account of the subversive spirit, 'Mayday' may be more rec-ognisable to you than some of the other stories I have shared with you today. We are all familiar with principles of prefigurative political action (Gayá & Brydon-Miller, 2017; Reinecke, 2018) as a framework for direct, local democratic action that became the foundation of our post-pandemic society. Well, this story represents one of the burgeoning local examples of collective subversion that arose at the height of neo-liberal hegemony. Considering the role of oppressive, normalised individualism in organisation, it is a testament to the subversive spirit of this collective that they constructed their own alternative organisational space (Callahan,

2013). With their network as a platform, they were able to build on existing shared parental demands for better working conditions for parents at work (Gatto, 2020). This collective action instigated a new type of 'family friendly' organisation grounded in the principles of flexibility (Fuller & Hirsh, 2019), justice and equity. Mayday represents the moment when the stories of individualised oppression that I have shared with you today were collectively harnessed and redirected into action by 'directly intervening in the ongoing reproduction of institutions' (Reinecke, 2018, p. 1300). Just as the notorious pandemic 'circuit breaker lockdowns' interrupted the reproduction of the virus, so did Mayday direct actions interrupt the continuous reproduction of patriarchal hegemony in organisations.

We must reflect on the PPE as a period of suffering for many parents at work, especially women. Though our present-day life has morphed into one of total flexibility and mutual care, it may only take another crisis to change this narrative again. We must preserve the humanity of our collective responsibility for equality, reciprocal care and interrelatedness. We live in an unprecedented era of care (Tronto, 2015) that re-wrote the ethical foundations of our once patriarchal society (French & Weis, 2000; Jordan, 2020; Pullen & Rhodes, 2015). To relinquish all that we have gained would be an insult to the memory of the countless lives lost during those devastating pandemic years. My message to you today is to hold onto our solidarity and the spirit of subversion; together, as parents at work and caregivers, we are so much stronger than we can imagine!

NARRATORS CLOSING REMARKS

There you have it, colleagues. What do you think? The seeds of subversion sown in that office were germinating all over the UK during the 2020s plague of pandemics. With small pockets of impassioned people, whose principles for parental justice stayed true, the wheels of change began to turn. Today, we celebrate the long haul that saw patriarchal workplaces finally wake up and listen to their workers. Should it have taken a global health and economic crisis to trigger this awakening? Absolutely not! But, if history has taught us anything, it is that crisis is also an opportunity to act. As we, today, face another potential creep backward towards the dark days of individualism and hegemonic masculinity, I ask you to steel yourselves for the fight and recall the experiences that your predecessors lived through. The narrative I have presented today is not a mere story, it is the lived experiences of parents at work and their experiences mattered then as much as they do now. I implore you to go forth into this conference with renewed passion for your filed and determination to protect the rights that were fought for and won over the last 100 years. Remember, they can all to easily be clawed back by those who would happily see a return to the patriarchal dividend.

And now, a final word from our sponsors...

REFERENCES

Abdellatif, A., & Gatto, M. (2020). It's OK not to be OK: Shared reflections from two PhD parents in a time of pandemic. *Gender, Work and Organization, 27*(5), 723–733. https://doi.org/10.1111/gwao.12465

Acker, J. (1990). Hierarchies, jobs, bodies: A theory of gendered organizations. *Gender & Society, 4*(2), 139–158.

Acker, J. (2006). Inequality regimes: Gender, class, and race in organizations. *Gender & Society, 20*(4), 441–464. https://doi.org/10.1177/0891243206289499

Acker, S., & Armenti, C. (2004). Sleepless in academia. *Gender and Education, 16*(1), 3–24.

Acker, S., & Dillabough, J. A. (2007). Women 'learning to labour' in the 'male emporium': Exploring gendered work in teacher education. *Gender and Education, 19*(3), 297–316. https://doi.org/10.1080/09540250701295460

Althusser, L. (2014). *On the reproduction of capitalism: Ideology and ideological state apparatuses.* Verso Trade.

Alvesson, M., & Due Billing, Y. (2009). *Understanding gender and organizations.* SAGE Publications. http://ebookcentral.proquest.com/lib/northumbria/detail.action?docID=537756

Amsler, S., & Motta, S. C. (2019). The marketised university and the politics of motherhood. *Gender and Education, 31*(1), 82–99. https://doi.org/10.1080/09540253.2017.1296116

Ashley, C. J., Jessica, & Hall, J. (2020). *Kinship carers' experiences during the coronavirus crisis.* https://www.frg.org.uk/images/Cross_party_PT_on_KC/Kinship_carers_experiences_report.pdf

Atwood, M. (1996). *The handmaid's tale* (New ed.). Vintage.

Atwood, M. (2019). *The testaments.* Chatto & Windus.

Bach, A. S. (2019). The ambiguous construction of nondominant masculinity: Configuring the "new" man through narratives of choice, involved fatherhood, and gender equality. *Men and Masculinities, 22*(2), 338–359. https://doi.org/10.1177/1097184x17715494

Bailey, J. (2015). Understanding contemporary fatherhood: Masculine care and the patriarchal deficit [Article]. *Families Relationships and Societies, 4*(1), 3–17. https://doi.org/10.1332/204674314x14036152282447

Beauvoir, S. D. (2011). *The second sex [Deuxième sexe].* Vintage Books.

Berdahl, J. L., & Moon, S. H. (2013). Workplace mistreatment of middle class workers based on sex, parenthood, and caregiving [Article]. *Journal of Social Issues, 69*(2), 341–366. https://doi.org/10.1111/josi.12018

Blackman, L. (2019). Haunted data, transmedial storytelling, affectivity: Attending to 'controversies' as matters of ghostly concern. *Ephemera, 19*(1), 31–52.

Bloom, P. N., & White, P. J. (2016). The moral work of subversion. *Human Relations, 69*(1), 5–31. https://doi.org/10.1177/0018726715576041

Bourdieu, P. (1989). Social space and symbolic power. *Sociological Theory, 7*(1), 14–25. https://doi.org/10.2307/202060

Bourdieu, P. (2001). *Masculine domination.* Polity Press.

Brandth, B., & Kvande, E. (2018). Masculinity and fathering alone during parental leave [Article]. *Men and Masculinities, 21*(1), 72–90. https://doi.org/1 0.1177/1097184x16652659

Brandth, B., & Kvande, E. (2019). Workplace support of fathers' parental leave use in Norway. *Community, Work & Family, 22*(1), 43–57. https://doi.org/1 0.1080/13668803.2018.1472067

Brearley, J. (2021). *Pregnant then screwed: The truth about the motherhood penalty and how to fix it.* Simon & Schuster, UK.

Bridges, T., & Pascoe, C. J. (2014). Hybrid masculinities: New directions in the sociology of men and masculinities. *Sociology Compass, 8*(3), 246–258. https://doi.org/10.1111/soc4.12134

Budig, M. J., & England, P. (2001). The wage penalty for motherhood. *American Sociological Review*, 204–225.

Bunting, M. (2020). *Labours of love: The crisis of care.* Granta Books.

Burgess, A. (1998). *Fatherhood reclaimed: The making of the modern father.* Random House.

Burgess, A., & Goldman, R. (2021). *Lockdown fathers: The untold story* (Contemporary fathers in the UK series, Issue).

Burnett, S., Gatrell, C., Cooper, C., & Sparrow, P. (2012). Fathers at work: A ghost in the organizational machine. *Gender, Work and Organization, 20*(6). https://doi.org/10.1111/gwao.12000

Butler, J. (2011). *Gender trouble: Feminism and the subversion of identity.* Routledge Ltd. https://www.dawsonera.com:443/abstract/9780203824979

Cahusac, E., & Kanji, S. (2014). Giving up: How gendered organizational cultures push mothers out [Article]. *Gender, Work and Organization, 21*(1), 57–70. https://doi.org/10.1111/gwao.12011

Callahan, J. L. (2013). 'Space, the final frontier'? Social movements as organizing spaces for applying HRD. *Human Resource Development International, 16*(3), 298–312.

Chesley, N. (2011). Stay-at-home fathers and breadwinning mothers: Gender, couple dynamics, and social change [Article]. *Gender & Society, 25*(5), 642–664. https://doi.org/10.1177/0891243211417433

Collier, R. (2019). Fatherhood, gender and the making of professional identity in large law firms: Bringing men into the frame [Article]. *International Journal of Law in Context, 15*(1), 68–87. https://doi.org/10.1017/s1744552318000162

Connell, R. (2003). *Gender and power: Society, the person and sexual politics.* Polity Press.

Connell, R. (2005). *Masculinities.* Polity Press.

Connell, R. (2021). *Gender: In world perspective.* Polity Press.

Correll, S. J., Benard, S., & Paik, I. (2007). Getting a job: Is there a motherhood penalty? *American Journal of Sociology, 112*(5), 1297–1338.

Crespi, I., & Ruspini, E. (2015). Transition to fatherhood: New perspectives in the global context of changing men's identities INTRODUCTION [Editorial material]. *International Review of Sociology-Revue Internationale De Sociologie, 25*(3), 353–358. https://doi.org/10.1080/03906701.2015.1078529

Demetriou, D. Z. (2001). Connell's concept of hegemonic masculinity: A critique. *Theory and Society, 30*(3), 337–361. http://www.jstor.org/stable/657965

Doucet, A. (2006a). *Do men mother?* University of Toronto Press.

Doucet, A. (2006b). 'Estrogen-filled worlds': Fathers as primary caregivers and embodiment [Article]. *The Sociological Review, 54*(4), 696–716. https://doi.org/10.1111/j.1467-954X.2006.00667.x

Eagly, A. H., & Karau, S. J. (2002). Role congruity theory of prejudice toward female leaders. *Psychological Review, 109*(3), 573–598. https://doi.org/10.1037/0033-295X.109.3.573

Eagly, A. H., Wood, W., & Diekman, A. B. (2000). Social role theory of sex differences and similarities: A current appraisal. *The Developmental Social Psychology of Gender, 12,* 174.

Elliott, K. (2016). Caring masculinities:Theorizing an emerging concept. *Men and Masculinities, 19*(3), 240–259. https://doi.org/10.1177/1097184x15576203

Fatherhood Institute. (2022). *Daddy leave: Why Britain's fathers need more time off work during their babies' first year* (A Fatherhood Institute briefing, Issue). http://www.fatherhoodinstitute.org/wp-content/uploads/2022/06/Daddy-Leave-Briefing-June-2022-1.pdf

Firestone, S. (1979). The dialectic of sex (Chapter 1). In *The dialectic of sex.* The Women's Press. https://www.marxists.org/subject/women/authors/firestone-shulamith/dialectic-sex.htm

Fodor, E., & Glass, C. (2018). Negotiating for entitlement: Accessing parental leave in Hungarian firms [Article]. *Gender, Work and Organization, 25*(6), 687–702. https://doi.org/10.1111/gwao.12208

Foucault, M. (1971). Orders of discourse. *Social Science Information, 10*(2), 7–30.

Foucault, M. (1978). *The history of sexuality: Volume I: An introduction.* Pantheon Books.

Freire, P. (2004). *Pedagogy of hope: Reliving pedagogy of the oppressed.* Bloomsbury Publishing.

Freire, P. (2017). *Pedagogy of the oppressed*. Penguin Classics.

French, W., & Weis, A. (2000). An ethics of care or an ethics of justice. *Journal of Business Ethics, 27*(1), 125–136. https://doi.org/10.1023/A:1006466520477

Fuller, S., & Hirsh, C. E. (2019). "Family-friendly" jobs and motherhood pay penalties: The impact of flexible work arrangements across the educational spectrum [Article]. *Work and Occupations, 46*(1), 3–44. https://doi.org/10.1177/0730888418771116

Gatrell, C. (2005). *Hard Labour: The sociology of parenthood, family life and career*. Open University Press. https://books.google.co.uk/books?id=F50eAQAAIAAJ

Gatto, M. (2020). Parenthood demands: Resisting a dystopia in the workplace. *Human Resource Development International, 23*(5), 569–585. https://doi.org/10.1080/13678868.2020.1735832

Gayá, P., & Brydon-Miller, M. (2017). Carpe the academy: Dismantling higher education and prefiguring critical utopias through action research. *Futures, 94*, 34–44. https://doi.org/10.1016/j.futures.2016.10.005

Gill, R. (2009). Breaking the silence: The hidden injuries of neo-liberal academia. In *Secrecy and silence in the research process: Feminist reflections* (pp. 228–244).

Gloor, J. L., Li, X., Lim, S., & Feierabend, A. (2018). An inconvenient truth? Interpersonal and career consequences of "maybe baby" expectations. *Journal of Vocational Behavior, 104*, 44–58. https://doi.org/10.1016/j.jvb.2017.10.001

Goldstein-Gidoni, O. (2020). Working fathers' in Japan: Leading a change in gender relations? *Gender, Work and Organization, 27*(3), 362–378. https://doi.org/10.1111/gwao.12380

Hanlon, N. (2012). *Masculinities, care and equality: Identity and nurture in men's lives*. Palgrave Macmillan.

Hattenstone, S. (2019). The dad who gave birth: 'Being pregnant doesn't change me being a trans man'. *The Guardian*. https://www.theguardian.com/society/2019/apr/20/the-dad-who-gave-birth-pregnant-trans-freddy-mcconnell

Hochschild, A. R. (1979). Emotion work, feeling rules, and social structure. *American Journal of Sociology, 85*(3), 551–575. https://doi.org/10.1086/227049

Hochschild, A. R. (1997). *The time bind: When work becomes home and home becomes work*. Metropolitan Books.

Hochschild, A. R., & Machung, A. (2012). *The second shift: Working families and the revolution at home*. Penguin Books Ltd.

Hojgaard, L. (1997). Working fathers – Caught in the web of the symbolic order of gender [Article]. *Acta Sociologica, 40*(3), 245–261. https://doi.org/10.1177/000169939704000302

Horne, R. M., & Breitkreuz, R. S. (2018). The motherhood sacrifice: Maternal experiences of child care in the Canadian context. *Journal of Family Studies*, *24*(2), 126–145. https://doi.org/10.1080/13229400.2015.1109540

Horton, M., Kohl, J., & Kohl, H. (1990). *The long haul* (Vol. 80). Doubleday.

Huffman, A. H., Olson, K. J., O'Gara, T. C., & King, E. B. (2014). Gender role beliefs and fathers' work-family conflict [Article]. *Journal of Managerial Psychology*, *29*(7), 774–793. https://doi.org/10.1108/jmp-11-2012-0372

Hunter, S. C., Augoustinos, M., & Riggs, D. W. (2017). Ideological dilemmas in accounts of primary caregiving fathers in Australian news media [Article]. *Discourse Context & Media*, *20*, 116–123. https://doi.org/10.1016/j.dcm.2017.09.005

Irigaray, L., & Gill, G. C. (1993). *An ethics of sexual difference*. Cornell University Press.

Jameson, F. (2010). Utopia as method, or uses of the future. In M. D. T. Gordin, Helen, & G. Prakash (Eds.), *Utopia/dystopia: Conditions of historical possibility* (pp. 21–44). Princeton University Press.

Jiao, M. (2019). MOTHERING AND MOTHERHOOD: EXPERIENCE, IDEOLOGY, AND AGENCY [Article]. *Comparative Literature Studies*, *56*(3), 541–556. https://doi.org/10.5325/complitstudies.56.3.0541

Jordan, A. (2020). Masculinizing care? Gender, ethics of care, and fathers' rights groups. *Men and Masculinities*, *23*(1), 20–41. https://doi.org/10.1177/1097184x18776364

Kangas, E., Lämsä, A. M., & Jyrkinen, M. (2019). Is fatherhood allowed? Media discourses of fatherhood in organizational life [Article]. *Gender, Work and Organization*. https://doi.org/10.1111/gwao.12352

Kaufman, G. (2018). Barriers to equality: Why British fathers do not use parental leave. *Community, Work & Family*, *21*(3), 310–325. https://doi.org/10.1080/13668803.2017.1307806

Kelland, J., Lewis, D., & Fisher, V. (2022). Viewed with suspicion, considered idle and mocked-working caregiving fathers and fatherhood forfeits. *Gender, Work and Organization*, *n/a*(n/a). https://doi.org/10.1111/gwao.12850

Kimmel, M. S., Hearn, J., & Connell, R. W. (2005). *Handbook of studies on men and masculinities*. Sage Publications.

Kvande, E., & Brandth, B. (2019). Designing parental leave for fathers–promoting gender equality in working life. *International Journal of Sociology and Social Policy*.

Lee, J. Y., & Lee, S. J. (2018). Caring is masculine: Stay-at-home fathers and masculine identity [Article; proceedings paper]. *Psychology of Men & Masculinity*, *19*(1), 47–58. https://doi.org/10.1037/men0000079

Maternity Action. (2020). *An equal endeavour? Maternity action's vision for replacing shared parental leave with a more equitable system of maternity and paternity leave*. https://maternityaction.org.uk/what-we-do/briefing-papers/

Messerschmidt, J. W. (2018). *Hegemonic masculinity: Formulation, reformulation, and amplification*. Rowman & Littlefield Publishers.

Messner, M. A. (1993). "Changing men" and feminist politics in the United States. *Theory and Society, 22*(5), 723–737. http://www.jstor.org/stable/657993

Miller, T. (2011). Falling back into gender? Men's narratives and practices around first-time fatherhood [Article]. *Sociology – THE Journal of the British Sociological Association, 45*(6), 1094–1109. https://doi.org/10.1177/0038038511419180

Mozziconacci, V. (2019). "The staff are academic": For a feminist subversion of the university, from pedagogy to the institution. *Gender, Sexuality & Society, 22*(Fall).

Munsch, C. L., Weaver, J. R., Bosson, J. K., & O'Connor, L. T. (2018). Everybody but me: Pluralistic ignorance and the masculinity contest [Article]. *Journal of Social Issues, 74*(3), 551–578. https://doi.org/10.1111/josi.12282

Murgia, A., & Poggio, B. (2009). Challenging hegemonic masculinities: Men's stories on gender culture in organizations [Article]. *Organization, 16*(3), 407–423. https://doi.org/10.1177/1350508409102303

Murgia, A., & Poggio, B. (2013). Fathers' stories of resistance and hegemony in organizational cultures [Article]. *Gender, Work and Organization, 20*(4), 413–424. https://doi.org/10.1111/j.1468-0432.2012.00592.x

Nardi, A. L., Frankenberg, A. D., & v., Franzosi, O. S., & Santo, L. C. d. E. (2020). Impact of institutional aspects on breastfeeding for working women: A systematic review. *Ciência & Saúde Coletiva, 25*, 1445–1462. http://www.scielo.br/scielo.php?script=sci_arttext&pid=S1413-81232020000401445&nrm=iso

Nayak, A., & Kehily, M. J. (2006). Gender undone: Subversion, regulation and embodiment in the work of Judith Butler. *British Journal of Sociology of Education, 27*(4), 459–472. http://www.jstor.org/stable/30036156

Noddings, N. (1995). Caring. In V. Held (Ed.), *Justice and care: Essential readings in feminist ethics* (pp. 7–31). Routledge.

Norman, H. (2020). Does paternal involvement in childcare influence mothers' employment trajectories during the early stages of parenthood in the UK? *Sociology, 54*(2), 329–345. https://doi.org/10.1177/0038038519870720

Norman, H., Elliot, M., & Fagan, C. (2014). Which fathers are the most involved in taking care of their toddlers in the UK? An investigation of the predictors of paternal involvement. *Community, Work & Family, 17*(2), 163–180. https://doi.org/10.1080/13668803.2013.862361

Özkazanç-Pan, B., & Pullen, A. (2020). Gendered labour and work, even in pandemic times. *Gender, Work and Organization, 27*(5), 675–676. https://doi.org/10.1111/gwao.12516

Palmer, Z. D. (2021). "I'm going to love and tolerate the shit out of you": Hybrid masculinities in the brony community. *Men and Masculinities*, 1097184X211031969.

Parker, M., & Jary, D. (1995). The McUniversity: Organization, management and academic subjectivity. *Organization, 2*(2), 319–338. https://doi.org/10.1177/135050849522013

Parker, M., & Starkey, K. (2018). Shut down business schools? Two professors debate. *The Conversation.* https://theconversation.com/shut-down-business-schools-two-professors-debate-96166

Perkins Gilman, C. (1915). *Herland.* Wisehouse Classics.

Peukert, A. (2017). Involved fathers between work and family life re/production of masculinity in negotiations within couples [Article]. *Zeitschrift Fur Familienforschung, 29*(1), 90–113. https://doi.org/10.3224/zff.v29i1.05

Pors, J. G., Olaison, L., & Otto, B. (2019). Ghostly matters in organizing. *Ephemera, 19,* 1–29.

Pullen, A., & Rhodes, C. (2015). Ethics, embodiment and organizations. *Organization, 22*(2), 159–165. https://doi.org/10.1177/1350508414558727

Randles, J. (2018). "Manning up" to be a good father: Hybrid fatherhood, masculinity, and U.S. responsible fatherhood policy. *Gender & Society, 32*(4), 516–539. https://doi.org/10.1177/0891243218770364

Reid, E. M. (2018). Straying from breadwinning: Status and money in men's interpretations of their wives' work arrangements. *Gender, Work and Organization, 25*(6), 718–733. https://doi.org/10.1111/gwao.12265

Reinecke, J. (2018). Social movements and prefigurative organizing: Confronting entrenched inequalities in occupy London. *Organization Studies, 39*(9), 1299–1321. https://doi.org/10.1177/0170840618759815

Shaw, K. (2018). *Hauntology : The presence of the past in twenty-first century english literature.* Springer International Publishing AG. http://ebookcentral.proquest.com/lib/northumbria/detail.action?docID=5355964

Sihto, T. (2015). Choosing to work? Mothers return-to-work decisions, social class, and the local labor market [Article]. *Nordic Journal of Working Life Studies, 5*(3), 23–40. https://doi.org/10.19154/njwls.v5i3.4805

Spitzmueller, C., Wang, Z. X., Zhang, J., Thomas, C. L., Fisher, G. G., Matthews, R. A., & Strathearn, L. (2016). Got milk? Workplace factors related to breastfeeding among working mothers [Article]. *Journal of Organizational Behavior, 37*(5), 692–718. https://doi.org/10.1002/job.2061

Stein, A. (2018). Professionalization and subversion. *Sexualities, 21*(8), 1243–1245. https://doi.org/10.1177/1363460718779215

Stock, A. (2016). The future-as-past in dystopian fiction [conceptual]. *Poetics Today, 37*(3), 415–442. https://doi.org/10.1215/03335372-3599495

Tronto, J. C. (2015). *Who cares? How to reshape a democratic politics* (1st ed.). Cornell University Press. http://www.jstor.org/stable/10.7591/j.ctt18kr598

Turner, P. K., & Norwood, K. (2014). 'I had the luxury…': Organizational breastfeeding support as privatized privilege. *Human Relations, 67*(7), 849–874. https://doi.org/10.1177/0018726713507730

von Alemann, A., Beaufays, S., & Oechsle, M. (2017). Involved fatherhood in work organizations sense of entitlement and hidden rules in organizational cultures [Article]. *Zeitschrift Fur Familienforschung, 29*(1), 72–89. https://doi.org/10.3224/zff.v29i1.04

Wall, G., & Arnold, S. (2007). How involved is involved fathering? An exploration of the contemporary culture of fatherhood [Article]. *Gender & Society, 21*(4), 508–527. https://doi.org/10.1177/0891243207304973

Weststar, J. (2012). Negotiating in silence: Experiences with parental leave in academia. *Relations industrielles / Industrial Relations, 67*(3), 352–374. https://doi.org/10.7202/1012535ar

Zhao, J., Wang, T., Yatskar, M., Ordonez, V., & Chang, K.-W. (2017). *Men also like shopping: Reducing gender bias amplification using corpus-level constraints.* arXiv preprint arXiv:1707.09457.

The Parental Club: 2029

Abstract This chapter is a speculative future online meeting between members of a national network for parents at work during a possible future where the world is plunged into another pandemic. Drawing on my lived experience in such networks during the COVID-19 pandemic, and the solidarity lifelines such networks offered to those in isolation, this chapter will focus on the conversation between members regarding the DeJa'Vu of parental inequity when the rhetoric of 'good enough is good enough' was not viewed as 'good enough' after the previous pandemic. Members tell their own stories of inequity and discuss their demands for necessary changes to organisational policy and culture for parents at work.

Keywords Policy • Culture • Subversion • Masculinities • Dystopian fictocriticism

> **Writing parents at work is writing care.**
> It's the everyday practical care for my children
> that slowly drains my energy and enthusiasm.
> Or the mutual care between my wife and I
> As we share our vulnerabilities and support each other.
> It's the relational care between colleagues,

Who offer empathy when times get tough.
It's the stoic care for my career and those
With whom I am interdependent.
And, it's the self-care of knowing when it's time to
Stop.

LOCKDOWN LOG-ON

'Hello?'

A quiet voice speaks into the void of a video call lobby. There is silence in a simulation lounge space where her head is hovering above an avatar body that is sitting, alone, on the central sofa, not a spot she would have chosen. The sofas are different styles, the one she finds herself occupying is a weathered faux-leather, while the others are pastille blue, grey, green and red. The room itself is partly obscured, but some inoffensive artworks are visible behind her head. It's different every time, apparently to conjure a sense of entering a boutique café. She looks down at her instant coffee with a wry smile and clicks her mouse. The lounge disappears and in its place, a web browser appears with 'X' loaded. The news feed is a frenetic flurry of fury and fear. #herewegoagain is trending alongside #antivax and #antilockdown. More clicks and the page scrolls down slowly, revealing promoted blue tick content. Another click and the 'following' page is displayed, replacing the 'for you'.

The messages are different here. She recognises the people she has come to know through their collective consciousnesses. This is where the network shared the impromptu social invitation. She didn't know how many would have seen it this morning, but she was primed having already spent three days in total isolation. She starts to scroll the feed.

> I'm scared. Last time we just about got through it, but this is terrifying. I'm just so scared for my baby. #zika29

> I heard Brazil knew about this 6 months ago but had a total comms lockdown #zika29 #Bolsomito

> #WHO would have thought that global heating and increased floods could lead to mosquitos in the UK? #zika29 #Climate

> Great, I get to watch my four walls for six months, while the stale male and pales get to walk the golf courses. Time for a bingewatch of #TheHandmaidsTale #zika29 #lockdown2.0

Her scrolling gets faster and her heart rate rises. The pain in her lower back gets louder and her ankles start to throb. She places her hand on her tummy and takes a deep, long breath in and out.

'*Hello Leni.*' A voice calls out from the laptop speaker.

Leni clicks the blue icon and the lounge reappears. She smiles as she recognises Naomi, who is inexplicably allocated a spot at the periphery of a separate soft blue sofa despite the clear spaces next to her.

'*Hey, Naomi.*' Leni replies, dragging her avatar to sit next to Naomi. They chuckle as they offer each other a virtual hug, which turns into a snort as the avatar animation renders Leni's hand through Naomi's shoulder blades and out through her chest, like an alien chest-buster.

'*How are you?*' Naomi asks as they continue the embrace, the animation resets and assumes a less disturbing, conventional visual.

'*Pretty bad to be honest.*'

'*Yeah, me too*'

'*I just don't know what's going to happen. I heard it might be mutating to airborne this morning.*'

'*Where did you hear that?*'

'*X*'

'*Stay away from that place. It's worse than ever! You know they are raking in the click and view profits, don't you?*' Naomi says as she releases the hug pose.

'*Yeah, I know. I just can't bear to watch the news and this is a way for me to participate.*'

'*I saw.*'

'*OK, maybe that was a mistake. I'm just so angry at my manager. I can't even say his name! No, I can't hand over my research project to a colleague. It's mine! Just because I'm stuck in my flat, doesn't mean I have to gift my hard work to someone else, just so the department can meet its annual research metric.*'

'*I agree, but maybe X wasn't the forum.*'

'*I know, I know… I've been summoned to a meeting tomorrow morning. Don't imagine we will be on sofas.*'

'*Shit. Do you have someone to go with you?*'

'*Yes, we have union reps in our network. I have already reached out to them. It's good to know they have my back.*'

Another face appears on the sofa where Leni had been. His avatar sits bolt upright with knees together and hands clasped at his lap. '*Hello Leni, hi Naomi. I thought I would be the first one here.*' He says with an exaggerated laugh.

'*Hi Kaz.*' Both Leni and Naomi reply.

'So, here we are again!' Kaz declares with a semi-smile.

'*Yep, here we are.*' Naomi and Leni reply in unison.

There is a pause and they each look at each other. In Leni's room, a clock ticks inexorably onwards, step by step unveiling the uncertain present before them. In its wake, thoughts and feelings fade away like briefly visible footprints on wet sand at the cusp of an advancing tide. As the clock ticks on, more faces appear on the sofas. Each smile and say hello in their own way. Many look heavy-eyed and their smiles border on grimaces. The avatars fill the spaces on the sofas and more sofas are generated automatically. The aspect ratio of the room expands to allow each person to be present in the shared space.

'*Thank you so much for being here, today.*' Naomi announces. '*We are not alone, we will go through this together. We are also not alone in our lived experience of parenthood in a pandemic. We have a wealth of stories to lean on, cry with, and smile to from COVID-19. Before we open the floor, I want to share some insights from* **The Care Manifesto** *by* The Care Collective

(2020) *that I know many of you have heard me discuss before. I propose we form a care community to help each other through the months ahead.'*
'*Here we go.'* A sarcastic voice interrupts.
'*Quiet!'* Another replies.
' *No, let him speak.'* Naomi declares. '*This is our space and we can't care for each other if people cannot speak their truth.'*
'*It's this utopian manifesto bullshit. It's all well and good to write some airy-fairy words on a page and dream of the wonderful society we will become, if only politicians and corporations would read it and have their **eureka** moment. It didn't work a decade ago, it won't work now. My immediate problems are the same as they were back then. I had two little ones when the pandemic hit, I was furloughed and then I got long COVID. I never properly returned to my old job. All I saw from our leaders was no plan, not enough PPE, social division and exploitation. How's a care manifesto going to help me?'*
'*I agree. It won't help you, but it might help us.'* Leni interjects.
Naomi continues, '*Let me start with your point about utopianism. The Care Manifesto is not a prescriptive destination, it's an invitation to do something radical, to engage in the process of change* (Fournier, 2002), *though it shouldn't be seen as radical, should it? We knew about the crisis of care during COVID* (Bunting, 2020), *and we did nothing. Now the crisis is compounded by a decade of broken promises on childcare and health, money siphoned off to private havens. I propose, first and foremost, that we **care** for each other.'* Naomi pauses. There is silence on the call. Leni notices her bump kicking and the plate of toast that was resting there slides off in seeming slow-motion before landing, butter side down on the carpet. She is torn between mourning the toast and stroking the bump.
Naomi continues in a more authoritative tone than before, '*Before I outline my proposal, I must take issue with your use of 'airy fairy'. The first principle I want us to consider in our care community is that of **ambivalence*** (The Care Collective, 2020, pp. 28–29). *As parents we all care for our children, our partners and some for elderly parents, family or friends. Care is a rewarding, but often self-nihilating duty. There are days when I feel like I'm disappearing, moments when I cannot bear to look at my son, especially when he is insisting upon making a rabbit house in the already appallingly messy sitting room. But, later that day, I lie next to him, read a story, and remember what it is I love so much about being his mum. Being a parent at work is a conflictual existence, from the extasy of announcing your happiest news, to the brutal confrontation with the first few weeks of sleeplessness and*

despair, to the growing bond, the first smiles, the cuddles, the chats. There are daily tantrums and circular battles, mealtime strife, and morning cajoling. Parenthood at work is about care, but it's not a warm, nourishing, transcendent care, it's ambivalence is writ-large on the faces of the dad dragging himself out of bed to soothe the crying baby at 3am. It's the mum weaning her baby and expressing in the toilets during her return to work. Care is hard and it's lonely at times. Our care community can be a space of solidarity and mutual care where we can be real and stop pretending. I propose we begin with this shared understanding so we can be kind to each other when the competing pressures of our paid and unpaid work are at loggerheads. I want to know what you think, shall we go around the room?'

Kaz clears his throat and has his virtual hand raised.

'Go ahead, Kaz. For those who don't know, Kaz is one of our founding members.' Leni says.

'Thanks, Leni, and thanks for starting us off, Naomi. I still can't believe we are here again. I'm here as a parent and an ally to those of you who are becoming parents. I know you are scared about what the next few months are going to mean. I became a Dad just before the last pandemic and I cared for my son during the first lockdown. I remember walking down the empty streets and conversing with myself about the possibility that society could break down. I remember my fear at not having a 'go bag'. I remember my obsessive daily review of the global cases and deaths report, and trying to calculate the ratios and demographics. I remember losing my humanity as I became progressively more reassured that it was not impacting children the way it was affecting the elderly. Why was this such a positive news story? I remember the weeks of lockdown and self-isolation when COVID landed on my desk. Work became squashed and squeezed into small bursts at the beginning, middle and end of the day. It was a time to learn what was really important in life, but sadly those lessons were only rhetorically embraced by many organisations, and soon forgotten when the banks and economy started to wobble. I am here in this community to lend my ear and my time. I have come through those years of unending series of sicknesses and shame. Now we face a period of waiting, of unknowing and uncertainty. We wait for the news to unravel like a tangled net that obscured the contents within. What will this time mean for us (Bailey & Suddaby, 2023)? *Will we be pressured to fill it, or can we take a breath and think differently? Will our managers care?'* He pauses to take a drink. Heads nod around the room and wait for him to continue.

*Who cares? I care! And, I **know** that you all do, too. It was that **knowing** when my little ones were small that made it possible to get through the toughest* *times. Our affective solidarity* (Vachhani & Pullen, 2019) *was a source of strength and a constant salve for the daily wounds of parenthood. I remember the rush to return to the old ways. Yes, we could work more from home, but this was a blessing and a curse. It stopped us being a community and we became more inward facing. I sometimes wonder if this was encouraged so willingly because it made us **less** together. As we enter this new unknown future, our expectations have been erased and our plans no longer exist. What **is** constant is the promise of care we can make to each other, that no matter what happens, we will be there for each other to moan and cry and listen and laugh. Care for parents at work is ambivalent, but it does not have to be suffered alone.'*

Another voice enters our headphones. *'Hello everyone, I'm Sam. I've got a four-year-old daughter and a baby due this month. I've not engaged much in the network before. I've always been reassured to know it was there, life and work have just gotten in the way. I remember starting work during the last pandemic, I was sitting on a sofa with my laptop, doing admin and analysing data. Work didn't change much for me. Deadlines stayed the same and there was a rapid return to business as usual when the offices opened up again, but with some flexibility. The thing I learned from that time that I think will be really important now is how important your line manager is.'*

There is a swell of agreement around the room with nodding heads and thumbs up emojis.

'I agree with Sam. After the last pandemic, I had a pretty boring job, but a really good line manager. I was looking for better jobs that were more me, but every time I mentioned my need for flexibility, they just shut up shop. I didn't fit, not as a single mum. For me, a line manager who applies the rules flexibly is so important. I sacrificed my career for that relationship and the flexibility it gave me. I couldn't have survived without it.'

'Thanks Meera, I see others agreeing with you around the room.' Leni says, having lowered her hand. *'I'm hearing two themes so far, **line managers and flexibility**. It's not a surprise. These are the same themes that came out of the last pandemic. I was so confident they would come up that I did some reading before this meeting to share some of what people were saying back then, so we can demand what should have been happening for a decade!'*

'We've come a long way when it comes to flexibility, but it has not been without pitfalls. The COVID lockdowns highlighted the risk of blurred lines between work and family life (Abdellatif & Gatto, 2020; Chung et al., 2020), *and the potential that some employers may seek to monitor staff within their homes* (Azer, 2021). *We have seen this risk become reality with many jobs entering the metaverse. The bullshitisation* (Graeber, 2019) *of post-pandemic*

jobs continued to prioritise time-served over outputs and creativity. Working from home and working flexibly in the day had a cost for parents, it came in the form of increased surveillance, especially from managers seeking to justify the time they were owed. It is because of this that I will focus on the managers and what remains a massive issue for our working lives.

*'Managers don't just need training in the 'skills' (Powell, 2020), they need better resourcing. Middle managers, the ones responsible for managing people, those we most commonly interact with every day, can be the most 'squeezed' for time and cognitive energy (Bevan & Cooper, 2021). Why is their time so squeezed, because **their** managers don't care. If they did, they would recognise the immeasurable, unpredictable complexity of caring for people at work. Not just sending mandatory training reminders and ticking the appraisal boxes every year. If line management was actually valued for the integral interdependent role it is within organisations, it would not just be an afterthought to the 'real' business of work, it would have the same value as the grants we win, bids we secure, the papers we produce or the reports we complete. So, yes, managers need to be trained, but the best training in the world will be fade like tears in the rain if people time is squeezed into nothingness.*

Don't get me wrong, training is definitely important, but how we train is up for discussion. Could we turn to fiction? Scholars in the past have extolled the virtues of reading fictions (Czarniawska-Joerges & De Monthoux, 1994) to better understand and learn from the nuances of positive and negative portrayals of fictional manager identities (Learmonth & Griffin, 2020), or learning critical perspectives on ethical practice in business to 'explore how we live' through reading fictional characters (Michaelson, 2016, p. 593) as a process that continues beyond the reading and can help us 'relate to their complex personalities' (Michaelson, 2016, p. 595). Such approaches may seem frivolous to the ruthless pragmatism of crisis times, but if such care had been taken to normalise the 'seam' (De Cock & Land, 2006) between everyday pressures and human emotion, perhaps we would be in a far more caring and compassionate position as we enter this crisis. Another perspective from the pre-pandemic was that of critical storytelling in and of organisations. Beigi et al. (2019) found that storytelling created a space for women's voices to flourish amidst masculine norms of writing and researching organisations. Could this process of feminising knowledge creation also apply to line managers?

One view coming out of that time was the 'androgynous manager' (Powell et al., 2021), or the importance of feminising the role and expectations of managers. As parents at work, we know what work-life imbalance feels like. Sadly, for many women, this is still their reality. It is the great irony of our time that the 'motherhood penalty' (Brearley, 2021) of stifled promotions or being 'managed out' of organisations, is a product of the ideal worker paradigm (Kelly et al., 2010; Rajan-Rankin, 2016) where the ideal is the segmented, cleansed, detached worker, who is a man. This 'ideal' contributes to the masculinity contest (Munsch et al., 2018) and a race to the bottom of maintaining the patriarchal organisational (Acker, 1990) through 'pluralistic ignorance' of the embedded inequities. We know that women leaders during the pandemic actually presided over fewer deaths (Kabeer et al., 2021), why was that ignored? The bullshitisation of our organisations is an ongoing maintenance of cultural masculinity that preserves the status quo. In fact, the wildfire of masculine-biased AI that scorched organisational communications across the western world in 2024 is exactly what I'm talking about as the maintenance of patriarchy.

*I envisage a more humane, caring approach to **'be human first'** and '**call out bad behaviour'** (Korica, 2022) as what a 'androgynous' or 'cyborg' (Haraway, 1991) manager could be. This would be a manager who behaves in the spirit of Ahmed's normalisation of 'complaint!' (Ahmed, 2021) and 'feminist killjoys' (Ahmed, 2010) where voicing the negative and representing the 'other' is something that is valued, not judged. Perhaps, bringing us back to ambivalent care, the manager we all need, whether human or AI, is a manager who shares our pain, who stands with us as we complain, who offers a shoulder to cry on, and perhaps sheds a tear of their own, too.'*

'James has his hand up, go on James.' Kaz says with a smile.

*'Hi everyone, I agree with what's been said so far. We still face a masculinity problem, but **what about dads** ? I know Zika29 is affecting pregnancies in ways we hadn't expected, and mums are rightly prioritised, but this is having a major impact upon my mental health, too. I know other expectant dads are feeling totally out of control right now. It was already bad for dads before COVID, being marginalised during pregnancy and childbirth (Dolan & Coe, 2011). COVID lockdowns were brutal, especially when dads were shut out of antenatal and perinatal appointments and even the birth (Fatherhood Institute, 2021). I'm scared this is going to happen again for me and my daughter. I want to be there when she arrives so she can see me and I can hold her. I have friends who still talk about missing the 20-week scan or watching through a phone screen. My line manager can't help with that.'*

'Go on, Tim' Leni interjects.

'*You're not alone, James. I was one of those COVID dads, and I only just made the birth having lost signal on my phone while sitting in the waiting room during labour. I still feel the heatsink when I saw the missed calls suddenly register and the text, 'where are you!'. I ran up those stairs and was incomprehensible as I blurted our my wife's name at reception. Thankfully, they got it. I often thing about the version of me that missed the birth, or the version of me who was with my wife through it all. I remember reading afterwards about the negative impact of insufficient policies upon young men becoming dads in the UK, and their transition into fatherhood* (Tarrant et al., 2022). *It was around that time that the Fatherhood Institute were campaigning for #timewithdad and the vital policy of paid, protected leave for fathers and partners in the first year* (Fatherhood Institute, 2022).*We were able to use the stats to prove the positive effect upon reducing the motherhood penalty and improving the first 1000 days for our children* (Norman, 2020; Norman et al., 2014). *We knew that we had to take the fight to the employers, because the state weren't interested. We got four weeks statutory from labour in 2028, didn't we? Hardly a radical vision of care in the UK. We don't really talk about it these days, but daddy leave is still a huge issue in the UK. It's funny that I can talk about these things here, but I feel gagged at work.*'

'Jose, you have your hand up.' Says Naomi. The energy in the lounge is increasing, more hands are rising and the looks on people's faces are bright and wide.

'*I feel the same, Tim. Finding a space where I can talk means everything to me. When we first started up the 'fathers forum'* (Kelland, 2022) *in this network, I wasn't sure how it would work. Over time, we have explored so many intimate stories of worry, hope and community. Books like 'Dad'* (Music. Football. Fatherhood, 2021) *gave us a way in to topics like birth trauma, miscarriage, gay fatherhood, interracial fatherhood, involved fatherhood, widowhood, divorce, estrangement, postnatal depression, and renewed passion for life. We needed the structure of topics at the start... To be honest, we still do. I'm always on the lookout for more stories of fatherhood to spark new conversations in the forum. COVID stories have certainly been a theme, but we have seen less and less of those in the last few years, I think people just choose to forget, or push the memories down inside. That's why this community is so important. We are all parents, we don't have the same experiences, and mums still have it worse than dads, but we are here, together.*'

'*Thanks Jose. Yes, this is why we're here, now, talking together and sharing what we know.*' Says Kaz, he has the head tilt down to a fine art and his warmth is palpable, even through a screen. '*Go ahead, Joseline*'

'*The problem is, there's so much written about COVID that we don't know where to start. What were the lessons for parents to take from that time. The embodied experiences in the feminist frontiers section of gender work and organisation* (Özkazanç-Pan & Pullen, 2020) *offer so much depth and emotion, but I feel swamped by it as I re-read the pain and suffering people went through. The 'never ending shift'* (Boncori, 2020) *of enforced flexible working for parents was a theme of that time wasn't it?*'

A chat message appears on the screen:

WE NEED TO TALK ABOUT SLEEP!

'*Go ahead, Stevie*' Says Naomi. There is an awkward pause as Stevie's screen appears. She starts talking, but we can't hear.

'*You're on mute, Stevie*' Says Naomi. There is a general flurry of laughter in the room that breaks the tension.

'*Sorry.*' Stevie's voice breaks free. '*Why is it that women manage the pressure of the patriarchal organisational by working harder and sleeping less* (Acker & Armenti, 2004). *Why am I the presumed lead role in night waking* (Borgkvist et al., 2020). *I was already losing hours of sleep as it was in my third trimester. This is going to be ridiculous if I'm also going to be doing home-schooling for my eldest.*'

'*It's not always the mums.*' James interjects.

'*That's correct, but please raise your hand to speak, James. Go on, Stevie.*' Naomi asserts.

'*I know it's not just women, but it's **most women** . When this lockdown kicks in, I'm worried that the caring rhetoric of 'good enough' will be replaced with 'not enough!', which will mean one thing for me and many other mums. Less sleep. The need to care won't go away, I can't speed up a tantrum or fast-track mealtime. It will be the sleep loss of parents in all organisations that will maintain the profits and productivity. Why should it take a crisis to talk about this issue?*'

'*You're right, Stevie.*' Says Leni. *This is why we're talking about this now. It's not right and we shouldn't have to repeat this message again and again, but that is our task.*'

Kaz raises his hand.

'Go ahead, Kaz' Says Naomi.

*'I wanted to take a moment to reflect on what I've been hearing so far. I think a lot of what we've been discussing relates to the **economics of care**. From undervaluing parental care, to exploiting sleep, and the role that dads should be playing in family life, it's clear that the current economics of patriarchal organisations only stack up for the patriarchal gender regime. I like what* Camilletti and Nesbitt-Ahmed (2022, p. 201) *said in the aftermath of COVID. They talked about the three Rs of recognising the unpaid labour that exists in domestic life, which underpins the patriarchal organisation, reducing the burden of that care by funding the infrastructure that enables it such as electricity, water etc., and finally redistributing the care of unpaid labour between all men and women, families and wider society. It's about confronting reality and dispelling the fiction of separate spheres. The paid economy that disproportionately favours men, is interdependent with the unpaid care economy of women caring for children and the elderly. We need to 'allocate resources that sustain and nurture these interdependencies; and to measure progress in ways that better reflect individual and societal well-being'* (Kabeer et al., 2021, p. 23).

'Can I add to that thought, Kaz?' Leni asks as she sits up in her chair. She feels the reflux of her buttered toast climbing up her gullet as she repositions her body. The acidity is distracting, but she wants to drive home this point.

'Sure, go ahead.' Kaz replies.

'I want to make a proposal for how we can build our community voice to capitalise on the scholarship that came out of the previous crisis. This Zika29 crisis has come knocking at the door of some of our most vulnerable, the babies in our wombs. We are the cradles of the future and we have a power we have not yet used. Rather than revising and resubmitting the same themes, I want us to think about how we can tell the existing story of a new caring economy. What if we took the universal economy (Chatzidakis et al., 2020) *seriously, through the common husbandry* (Nelson, 2016) *of our communities. We could focus on teaching boys caring masculinities* (Elliott, 2016). *We could argue for the shorter working week that prioritises caring for children, so those who do paid care can also spend time with their own children at the end of the day. We should be arguing for an end to the outsourcing and exploitation of care. As* De Henau and Himmelweit (2021) *proved, the investment in care is an investment in the whole workforce with benefits that outstrip the traditional construction focus of a patriarchal economy. It's time to be radical. It's time for care.*

I want to leave you with this to think about. What if we didn't wait for a crisis to revalue care? What if care was valued today and tomorrow? What if we organised on the shared belief in mutual care? What would that look like, today. How could that have helped us be prepared for what we face now?'

*   *   *

Writing parents at work is writing complaint.
It's writing to the HR helpline to find the policy,
Any policy.
It's moaning to colleagues about the time lost, again.
It's speaking to the manager about the parenting room
They promised 12 months ago.
It's working with the union to push for better rights.
It's being the voice in the room that repeats and repeats,
And repeats.
It's killing joy.

*   *   *

'*Being the collective voice is what gives us power.*' Leni says.
Kaz raised his hand with a grin. '*Yes, look at what we achieved as a collective in 2027. A commitment from every university across the UK to invest in parents and carers rooms in each of their campuses. Who would have thought that breastfeeding would become so normal in the workplace? Signs that say 'we are a family friendly campus' are commonplace now. I know there have been comments and many complaints, but we've opened pandora's box now and it's not going to close on our watch.*'
    '*I know we've seen backlash, especially from the manosphere* (Bates, 2020). *Now is the time to double down on the progress. Returning to the theme of ambivalent care, I thought we could use the remainder of today's meeting to reflect on the intersectional 'feminist commons'* (Mandalaki & Fotaki, 2020; Ticktin, 2021) *principles that brought us together. I'm speaking of the five Rs that represent our values as a network:*

RESPONSIBILITY, REFLEXIVITY, RESONANCE, RELATIONALITY AND RESISTANCE!

Naomi takes control of the meeting, '*We shout about unpaid labour* (Federici, 2021), *the undervalued labour that enables everyday life to continue. We shout about the exploitation of care and those sacrificed on the altar of productivity. We shout about the erasure of care in patriarchal organisational discourse. What do these five Rs mean for us today?*

Responsibility *means we are self-critical. We seek honesty and integrity in our actions. When we ask for your views, we treat them all with respect. We generate our narratives responsibly and with rigour to honour the emotion that is invested in the embodied experiences we are holding as our tools to represent parents at work.*

Reflexivity *means we place care first in our ethical approach to organising. We care for each other as an organisational ethics that reminds us of our interdependence as peers and friends. The unpaid care work we do is often left uncounted, yet it exists and we must value it and support each other. We don't have all the answers, we don't claim to. What we do have is our collective, affective solidarity and the awareness of where our strength lies.*

Resonance *means we constantly seek the intersectional stories of and for our members that speak to their lived experience and of those we want to reach. Our network takes responsibility for the diversity of its membership* (Dennissen et al., 2019, 2020), *we do not shy away from our privilege and we constantly seek feedback and reflection on who to better represent our members. These are the mums and dads, the guardians and adoptive parents whose lived experiences have been muted* (Calás & Smircich, 2020; Kissack, 2010) *by patriarchal discourse and the ghost of masculinity hiding around every corner. Our stories are shared so we can 'unmute' the marginalised and bridge the divide between parental isolation in work and the fear of being othered by a system that demands the ideal.*

Relationality *means that we are not bound by masculine rules of engagement. We transgress existing boundaries* (Grafström & Jonsson, 2020) *and spread our network like a the beautiful wilderness amongst the rigid towers and concrete jungle of western organisations. We refuse the essentialism of gender roles and embrace the incongruity of involved fathers* (Eagly & Karau, 2002).

Resistance *means we protest, we campaign, we complain, and we refuse to be muted. We spread our message and share the care* (Brooks & Hodkinson, 2021). *We won't be silenced and we won't perform mild subversion to maintain the status quo in patriarchal organisations* (Bloom & White, 2016). *We won't remain backstage actors who drag our heels and mutter behind closed doors* (Ybema & Horvers, 2017). *Our resistance will begin in our here* *and now with how we organise as a community of care. Care is our number one priority and all decisions will flow from it. Only by centring care can we subvert exploitation.*

'So, what next?' Kaz asks.

* * *

The screen freezes.
Leni tries to reconnect. She closes the window and reopens the link. Nothing. She feels her heart pumping in her chest. There is a loud unison of car and home alarms bouncing around the neighbourhood. *Strange* she thinks, that normally only happens with a power outage. She slowly lifts her body upright and peers out of the window. She sees a fly buzzing by the open slither of the sash window and slams it shut. She knows the virus is in mosquitos, but she can't help the fear. Outside she sees a man holding his phone up in the air. He's doing that futile waving gesture that people do when they are searching for signal.

Her neighbour, Lucy, has also stepped outside. She's on the phone, 'it's not working' she says as she throws her head back in despair. 'What do you mean 'nothing's working?' she shouts into the receiver.

Leni moves back from the window, she pulls the blinds down and sits at her desk. Her hand starts to shake. She reaches over to the cup of cold tea and takes a long gulp. Her screen is flickering with error messages, 'error23, cannot sync'. Then another message pops up:

WELCOME TO THE CLOUD CRASH. WELCOME TO THE FUTURE.

It lingers for a moment and she fumbles with her phone to try to take a picture, but it disappears before she can get the screen unlocked.

A text message appears on her screen. It's a novelty these days.

From Naomi: Hey, I found your number in my contacts. I hope this works. Did you get a screen message? I think the clouds have crashed...

Leni: Yes, it must be global.

Naomi: What do we do now?

CODA

The subversion of this dystopian fictocriticism is built upon the necessity of resisting the patriarchal discourse that is reproduced through interpellation and subjugates parental care within organisations. Though Althusser (2014) theorised interpellation as a totalising effect whereupon all individuals are always already subjects of ideology, such complete ownership of the consciousness of human beings is disputed by Butler (1997) and Dolar (1993) who suggested that there is always a 'remainder', or something left over from this process. They propose that this could be the intangible quality of **love** as an irreducible and nebulous quality of *being* a human, something not easily tied to social or structural phenomena i.e. outside of the patriarchal organisation. Taking Sartre's theorising of nothingness into consideration, it is also possible to consider the subversion of patriarchal interpellation through the lens of temporal consciousness:

> The future is what I would be if I were not free and what I can have to be only because I am free. It appears on the horizon to announce to me what I am from the standpoint of what I shall be. (Sartre, 2003, p. 151)

Our futures do not yet exist, they creep towards us on an approaching array of horizons. Some will come into view as we step beyond, others will be nihilated by our own choices, or the social events around us. For parents at work, we can have a role in shaping the future we head towards. Our being need not be defined by the stereotype or social roles. We can choose to exist outside of that totalising process. Our community of care is an organisation in waiting, a future we can co-create by nihilating the version of ourselves that resists the resistance.

REFERENCES

Abdellatif, A., & Gatto, M. (2020). It's OK not to be OK: Shared reflections from two PhD parents in a time of pandemic. *Gender, Work and Organization, 27*(5), 723–733. https://doi.org/10.1111/gwao.12465

Acker, J. (1990). Hierarchies, jobs, bodies: A theory of gendered organizations. *Gender & Society, 4*(2), 139–158.

Acker, S., & Armenti, C. (2004). Sleepless in academia. *Gender and Education, 16*(1), 3–24.

Ahmed, S. (2010). Killing joy: Feminism and the history of happiness. *Signs, 35*(3), 571–594. https://doi.org/10.1086/648513

Ahmed, S. (2021). *Complaint!* Duke University Press.

Althusser, L. (2014). *On the reproduction of capitalism: Ideology and ideological state apparatuses.* Verso Trade.

Azer, E. (2021). Remote working has led to managers spying more on staff – Here are three ways to curb it. *The Conversation.* https://theconversation.com/remote-working-has-led-to-managers-spying-more-on-staff-here-are-three-ways-to-curb-it-159604

Bailey, C., & Suddaby, R. (2023). When time falls apart: Re-centering human time in organisations through the lived experience of waiting. *Organization Studies, 0*(ja), 01708406231166807. https://doi.org/10.1177/01708406231166807

Bates, L. (2020). *Men who hate women: From incels to pickup artists, the truth about extreme misogyny and how it affects us all.* Simon and Schuster.

Beigi, M., Callahan, J. L., & Michaelson, C. (2019). A critical plot twist: Changing characters and foreshadowing the future of organizational storytelling. *International Journal of Management Reviews, 0*(0). https://doi.org/10.1111/ijmr.12203

Bevan, S., & Cooper, C. L. (2021). Is your manager bad for your health? In *The healthy workforce* (pp. 89–112). Emerald Publishing Limited. https://doi.org/10.1108/978-1-83867-499-120211004

Bloom, P. N., & White, P. J. (2016). The moral work of subversion. *Human Relations, 69*(1), 5–31. https://doi.org/10.1177/0018726715576041

Boncori, I. (2020). The never-ending shift: A feminist reflection on living and organizing academic lives during the coronavirus pandemic. *Gender, Work and Organization, 27*(5), 677–682. https://doi.org/10.1111/gwao.12451

Borgkvist, A., Eliott, J., Crabb, S., & Moore, V. (2020). "Unfortunately I'm a massively heavy sleeper": An analysis of fathers' constructions of parenting. *Men and Masculinities, 23*(3–4), 680–701. https://doi.org/10.1177/1097184x18809206

Brearley, J. (2021). *Pregnant then screwed: The truth about the motherhood penalty and how to fix it.* Simon & Schuster.

Brooks, R., & Hodkinson, P. (2021). *Sharing care: Equal and primary carer fathers and early years parenting.* Bristol University Press.

Bunting, M. (2020). *Labours of love: The crisis of care.* Granta Books.

Butler, J. (1997). "Conscience doth make subjects of us all": Althusser's subjection. In *The psychic life of power: Theories in subjection* (pp. 106–131). Stanford University Press.

Calás, M. B., & Smircich, L. (2020). Mute, mutation, and mutiny: On the work of feminist epistemology. *Journal of Management History.*

Camilletti, E., & Nesbitt-Ahmed, Z. (2022). COVID-19 and a "crisis of care": A feminist analysis of public policy responses to paid and unpaid care and domestic work [https://doi.org/10.1111/ilr.12354]. *International Labour Review, 161*(2), 195–218. https://doi.org/10.1111/ilr.12354

Chatzidakis, A., Hakim, J., Littler, J., Rottenberg, C., & Segal, L. (2020). From carewashing to radical care: The discursive explosions of care during Covid-19. *Feminist Media Studies, 20*(6), 889–895. https://doi.org/10.1080/1468077 7.2020.1781435

Chung, H., Seo, H., Forbes, S., & Birkett, H. (2020). *Working from home during the COVID-19 lockdown: Changing preferences and the future of work.* https:// kar.kent.ac.uk/83896/

Czarniawska-Joerges, B., & De Monthoux, P. (1994). *Good novels, better management: Reading organizational realities in fiction.* Routledge.

De Cock, C., & Land, C. (2006). Organization/literature: Exploring the seam. *Organization Studies, 27*(4), 517–535.

De Henau, J., & Himmelweit, S. (2021). A care-led recovery from covid-19: Investing in high-quality care to stimulate and rebalance the economy. *Feminist Economics, 27*(1–2), 453–469. https://doi.org/10.1080/1354570 1.2020.1845390

Dennissen, M., Benschop, Y., & van den Brink, M. (2019). Diversity networks: Networking for equality? *British Journal of Management, 30*(4), 966–980. https://doi.org/10.1111/1467-8551.12321

Dennissen, M., Benschop, Y., & van den Brink, M. (2020). Rethinking diversity management: An intersectional analysis of diversity networks. *Organization Studies, 41*(2), 219–240. https://doi.org/10.1177/0170840618800103

Dolan, A., & Coe, C. (2011). Men, masculine identities and childbirth [Article]. *Sociology of Health & Illness, 33*(7), 1019–1034. https://doi. org/10.1111/j.1467-9566.2011.01349.x

Dolar, M. (1993). Beyond interpellation. *Qui Parle, 6*(2), 75–96. http://www. jstor.org/stable/20685977

Eagly, A. H., & Karau, S. J. (2002). Role congruity theory of prejudice toward female leaders. *Psychological Review, 109*(3), 573–598. https://doi.org/1 0.1037/0033-295X.109.3.573

Elliott, K. (2016). Caring masculinities:Theorizing an emerging concept. *Men and Masculinities, 19*(3), 240–259. https://doi.org/10.117 7/1097184x15576203

Fatherhood Institute. (2021). *Dads shut out: Fathers and maternity services during the pandemic.* http://www.fatherhoodinstitute.org/2021/dads-shut-out-fathers-and-maternity-services-during-the-pandemic/

Fatherhood Institute. (2022). *Daddy leave: Why Britain's fathers need more time off work during their babies' first year* (A Fatherhood Institute briefing, Issue). http://www.fatherhoodinstitute.org/wp-content/uploads/2022/06/ Daddy-Leave-Briefing-June-2022-1.pdf

Federici, S. (2021). *Patriarchy of the wage: Notes on Marx, gender, and feminism*. PM Press.

Fournier, V. (2002). Utopianism and the cultivation of possibilities: Grassroots movements of hope. *The Sociological Review, 50*(1_suppl), 189–216.

Graeber, D. (2019). *Bullshit jobs: The rise of pointless work, and what we can do about it*. Penguin.

Grafström, M., & Jonsson, A. (2020). When fiction meets theory: Writing with voice, resonance, and an open end. In A. Pullen, J. Helin, & N. Harding (Eds.), *Writing differently* (Vol. 4, pp. 113–129). Emerald Publishing Limited. https://doi.org/10.1108/S2046-607220200000004007

Haraway, D. (1991). A cyborg manifesto: Science, technology, and socialist-feminism in the late twentieth century. In D. Haraway (Ed.), *Simians, cyborgs and women: The reinvention of nature* (pp. 190–233). Routledge.

Kabeer, N., Razavi, S., & van der Meulen Rodgers, Y. (2021). Feminist economic perspectives on the COVID-19 pandemic. *Feminist Economics, 27*(1–2), 1–29. https://doi.org/10.1080/13545701.2021.1876906

Kelland, J. (2022). *Caregiving fathers in the workplace: Organisational experiences and the fatherhood forfeit*. Springer International Publishing AG. http://ebookcentral.proquest.com/lib/northumbria/detail.action?docID=6951423

Kelly, E. L., Ammons, S. K., Chermack, K., & Moen, P. (2010). Gendered challenge, gendered response: Confronting the ideal worker norm in a white-collar organization. *Gender & Society, 24*(3), 281–303. https://doi.org/10.1177/0891243210372073

Kissack, H. (2010). Muted voices: A critical look at e-male in organizations. *Journal of European Industrial Training, 34*(6), 539–551.

Korica, M. (2022). A hopeful manifesto for a more humane academia. *Organization Studies, 0*(0), 01708406221106316. https://doi.org/10.1177/0170840 6221106316

Learmonth, M., & Griffin, M. (2020). Fiction and the identity of the manager. In *The Oxford handbook of identities in organizations*.

Mandalaki, E., & Fotaki, M. (2020). The bodies of the commons: Towards a relational embodied ethics of the commons. *Journal of Business Ethics, 166*(4), 745–760. https://doi.org/10.1007/s10551-020-04581-7

Michaelson, C. (2016). A novel approach to business ethics education: Exploring how to live and work in the 21st century. *Academy of Management Learning & Education, 15*(3), 588–606.

Munsch, C. L., Weaver, J. R., Bosson, J. K., & O'Connor, L. T. (2018). Everybody but me: Pluralistic ignorance and the masculinity contest [Article]. *Journal of Social Issues, 74*(3), 551–578. https://doi.org/10.1111/josi.12282

Music. Football. Fatherhood. (2021). *Dad: Untold stories of fatherhood, love, mental health and masculinity*.

Nelson, J. A. (2016). Husbandry: A (feminist) reclamation of masculine responsibility for care. *Cambridge Journal of Economics, 40*(1), 1–15.

Norman, H. (2020). Does paternal involvement in childcare influence mothers' employment trajectories during the early stages of parenthood in the UK? *Sociology, 54*(2), 329–345. https://doi.org/10.1177/0038038519870720

Norman, H., Elliot, M., & Fagan, C. (2014). Which fathers are the most involved in taking care of their toddlers in the UK? An investigation of the predictors of paternal involvement. *Community, Work & Family, 17*(2), 163–180. https://doi.org/10.1080/13668803.2013.862361

Özkazanç-Pan, B., & Pullen, A. (2020). Gendered labour and work, even in pandemic times. *Gender, Work and Organization, 27*(5), 675–676. https://doi.org/10.1111/gwao.12516

Powell, G. N. (2020). Work–family lockdown: Implications for a post-pandemic research agenda. *Gender in Management: An International Journal, 35*(7/8), 639–646. https://doi.org/10.1108/GM-05-2020-0148

Powell, G. N., Butterfield, D. A., & Jiang, X. (2021). The "good manager" over five decades: Towards an androgynous profile? *Gender in Management: An International Journal, 36*(6), 714–730. https://doi.org/10.1108/GM-01-2021-0023

Rajan-Rankin, S. (2016). Paternalism and the paradox of work-life balance: Discourse and practice [Article]. *Community, Work & Family, 19*(2), 227–241. https://doi.org/10.1080/13668803.2016.1134131

Sartre, J.-P. (2003). *Being and nothingness: An essay on phenomenological ontology.* Routledge.

Tarrant, A., Ladlow, L., Johansson, T., Andreasson, J., & Way, L. (2022). The impacts of the covid-19 pandemic and lockdown policies on young fathers: Comparative insights from the UK and Sweden. *Social Policy and Society, 1*–11. https://doi.org/10.1017/S1474746422000586

The Care Collective. (2020). *The care manifesto: The politics of interdependence.* Verso.

Ticktin, M. (2021). Building a feminist commons in the time of COVID-19. *Signs: Journal of Women in Culture and Society, 47*(1), 37–46. https://doi.org/10.1086/715445

Vachhani, S. J., & Pullen, A. (2019). Ethics, politics and feminist organizing: Writing feminist infrapolitics and affective solidarity into everyday sexism. *Human Relations, 72*(1), 23–47. https://doi.org/10.1177/0018726718780988

Ybema, S., & Horvers, M. (2017). Resistance through compliance: The strategic and subversive potential of frontstage and backstage resistance. *Organization Studies, 38*(9), 1233–1251. https://doi.org/10.1177/0170840617709305

APPENDIX 1: DYSTOPIAN FICTION TROPES AND INTERSECTING THEMES

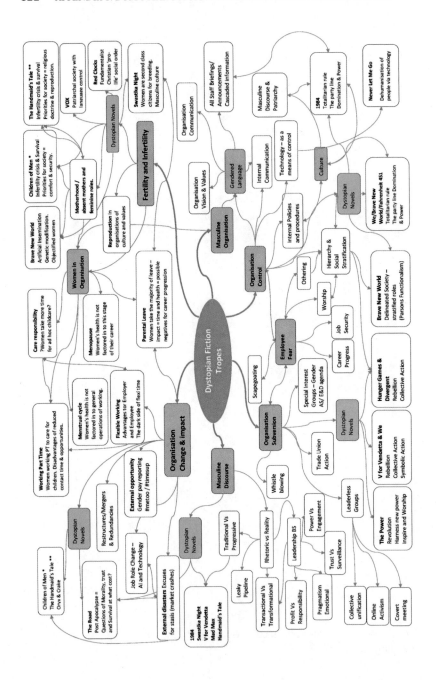

APPENDIX 2: PARTICIPANT SUMMARY TABLE

Demographics and parental information	Men	Women
Total	10	9
Ethnicity	9 White	8 White
	1 Black	1 Black
Working pattern	9 FT/1 PT	4 FT/5 PT (1 used AL to achieve 80% working for 12 months on return to work.)
Parental leave (for the purposes of this table, I use the policy title to describe the leave taken, e.g. maternity and paternity)	• 7–2 weeks paternity • 1–2 weeks paternity + 1 week AL • 1–2 weeks paternity + 2 weeks AL • 1 negotiated circa 8 working days absence from work due to less than 6 months service	• 5–12 months maternity + 2 months AL • 5–12 months maternity • 1–11 months maternity • 1–10 months maternity • 1–6 months maternity + 1 month AL
Childcare (note added when based on expectations)	• 1 FT nursery (expectations) • 1 mother full time with some family help • 1 nursery 4 days per week (expectations) • 4 nursery 3 days per week, 2 days with mother (1 based on expectations) • 1 nursery 3 days per week, 2 days shared between grandparents and parents (expectations) • 1 nursery 2 days per week, 2 days shared between parents, 1 day with grandparent • 1 nursery 2 days per week, 3 days shared between grandparents and parents (expectations)	

M. Gatto, *Parents at Work*,
https://doi.org/10.1007/978-3-031-15482-9

APPENDIX 3: CHARACTER AND THEME MAPPING

M. Gatto, *Parents at Work*,
https://doi.org/10.1007/978-3-031-15482-9

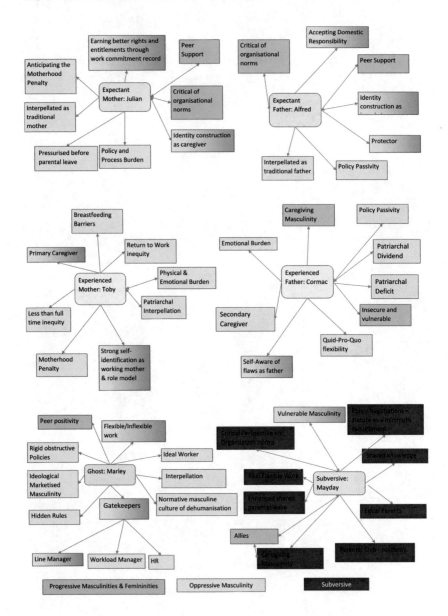

Some Recommended Dystopian/Ustopian Fictions

Alderman, N. (2016). *The power*. Penguin.

Atwood, M. (1996). *The Handmaid's tale* (New ed.). Vintage.

Atwood, M. (2014). *The MaddAddam trilogy bundle: The year of the flood; Oryx & Crake; MaddAddam*. Anchor.

Atwood, M. (2019). *The testaments*. Chatto & Windus.

Bradbury, R. (2012). *Fahrenheit 451: A novel*. Simon and Schuster.

Burdekin, K. (1985). *Swastika night*. The Feminist Press.

Butler, O. (2014). *Parable of the sower*. Four Walls Eight Windows.

Cook, D. (2020). *The new wilderness*. Oneworld Publications.

Dalcher, C. (2018). *Vox*. HarperCollins Publishers Limited.

Dalcher, C. (2020). *Q*. HQ.

Elison, M. (2016). *The book of the unnamed midwife*. 47North.

Huxley, A. (2004). *Brave new world*. Vintage Publishing.

Ishiguro, K. (2005). *Never let me go*. Faber and Faber.

Ishiguro, K. (2021). *Klara and the Sun: A novel*. Vintage.

James, P. D. (2018). *The children of men*. Faber & Faber.

Lunde, M. (2017). *The history of bees*. Simon and Schuster.

McCarthy, C. (2009). *The road*. Macmillan.

Orwell, G. (2004). *1984 nineteen eighty-four*. Penguin Modern Classics.

Sedgwick, H. (2019). *The growing season*. Vintage Publishing.

Zumas, L. (2018). *Red clocks* (ePub ed.). Little Brown & Company.

© The Author(s), under exclusive license to Springer Nature Switzerland AG 2023
M. Gatto, *Parents at Work*,
https://doi.org/10.1007/978-3-031-15482-9

INDEX

Printed in the United States
by Baker & Taylor Publisher Services